LECTURES ON THE HISTORY
OF THE PAPAL CHANCERY

LECTURES ON THE HISTORY
OF THE PAPAL CHANCERY

DOWN TO THE TIME OF INNOCENT III

by

REGINALD L. POOLE, Hon. Litt.D.

Sometime Birkbeck Lecturer in Ecclesiastical History at Trinity College

Keeper of the Archives of the University of Oxford, and Fellow of St Mary
Magdalen College and of the British Academy; LL.D., Edinburgh

Cambridge:
at the University Press
1915

CAMBRIDGE UNIVERSITY PRESS
Cambridge, New York, Melbourne, Madrid, Cape Town,
Singapore, São Paulo, Delhi, Mexico City

Cambridge University Press
The Edinburgh Building, Cambridge CB2 8RU, UK

Published in the United States of America by Cambridge University Press, New York

www.cambridge.org
Information on this title: www.cambridge.org/9781107622647

First published 1915
First paperback edition 2013

A catalogue record for this publication is available from the British Library

ISBN 978-1-107-62264-7 Paperback

PREFACE

THE study of Papal documents has occupied me for many years. I began transcribing Bulls during the time when I held a post in the Department of Manuscripts in the British Museum so long ago as 1880, but I do not think that I published anything on the subject until 1892. At that time my interest was mainly historical and palaeographical, but when in 1897 I was called upon to give regular instruction in diplomatic in my own University of Oxford, I was led to pay closer attention to the forms of documents and to the modes of their transmission; and since then in most years I have given either a full course of lectures, or, if time did not permit, at least a shorter series, on the history of the Papal Chancery and on the characteristics of its literary productions. I welcomed therefore the opportunity, offered by my election by the Master and Fellows of Trinity College to the Birkbeck Lectureship in Ecclesiastical History in 1912, for applying myself to the improvement and extension of my lectures; and after I had completed my course in the Michaelmas Term of 1913 I looked forward to recasting what I had written so as to form a methodical treatise on the subject. In this hope I have been disappointed. An infirmity of eyesight for many months made it very difficult for me to perform my ordinary tasks and precluded the possibility of rearranging the materials of my book, filled as it is with small details which would certainly have become confused had they been transferred and reinserted in different places without a more exact supervision than I could command. I was therefore obliged to leave the scheme of the work as it was at first composed, but I have done my best to revise the matter. I have rewritten nearly one-half of it, and have enlarged the book by about two-thirds. Originally it consisted of six lectures; but I removed some parts of the sixth and expanded them so as to form a seventh chapter. It was perhaps rash in the circumstances to venture upon publication at all; but I may plead in excuse that a book on the subject of which I treat is really wanted, for nothing at all dealing with it has ever been published in English. For this reason it will not be out of place to glance briefly at the course of its exposition in modern times.

The study of Papal as of other documents was founded in France. It is a part of the great learned tradition of the Benedictines of the congregation of St Maur. The illustrious Jean Mabillon first laid down the principles of diplomatic with a sureness of grasp which has made his treatise the model on which all subsequent work has proceeded. He had an instinct of critical divination which seldom allowed him to go astray, and the little that he says about Papal documents is pregnant with suggestions which have been turned to account by later scholars. His successors, the two authors of the Nouveau Traité de Diplomatique[1], dealt with the subject with much

---

[1] Their modesty forbade them from giving their names, but the survivor (R. T. Tassin) mentioned that of his colleague, Charles Toustain, in the preface to volume vi.

greater fulness. They may irritate us by their prolixity and by their constant attitude of defence against forgotten opponents; but their industry is beyond all praise, and the mass of material which they collected, especially with regard to the Papal Chancery, can never be neglected. But it would be idle to compare their critical initiative with that of Mabillon.

Nearly a century passed before a notable landmark in the study of Papal documents was fixed, in a Memoir on the Acts of Innocent III, by Léopold Delisle, a true successor of Mabillon in a large part of his varied activity. This short article, published in 1858, stands as the pattern for the exposition of the system of the Chancery and of the diplomatic of the later middle ages. Delisle's method is perfect; the main lines which he established have been established once for all, and even in details few of his statements have needed revision. His influence is apparent in the productions of the French School at Rome[1]; but these, if we except the important editions of the Liber Pontificalis and the Liber Censuum, have been mainly occupied with the documents of a more recent period than that to which this volume is confined.

During the eighteenth century there was great and continuous activity in Italy in the publication of materials for history, and especially for ecclesiastical history, but less interest was shown in the criticism of documents.

---

[1] This is not less true of the late Comte L. de Mas-Latrie's Éléments de la Diplomatique Pontificale, which appeared in the Revue des Questions Historiques xxxix. (1886) 415–451; and of the relative sections in Arthur Giry's Manuel de Diplomatique, 1894. It is incorrect to speak, with Dr Bresslau, Urkundenlehre, p. 31, of Giry having emancipated himself from the Maurine influence and worked in close connexion with German researches; for Giry, like Delisle, was unfamiliar with the German language.

Pierluigi Galletti in his book on the Primicerius furnished a storehouse of evidence bearing upon the early organization of the Chancery, and in 1805 Gaetano Marini produced an invaluable collection of documents preserved, or once preserved, on papyrus. But little was done in the way of constructive treatment. The Diplomatica Pontificia of Marino Marini, nephew of Gaetano, is an insipid and superficial sketch, based chiefly on the Nouveau Traité and only of interest for its occasional references to the Papal Registers. Until the Archives were thrown open by Pope Leo XIII in 1881 access to them was rarely permitted to anyone outside the official staff. The exceptional facilities granted to the Danish historian P. A. Munch in 1860 resulted in the production of the first scientific treatise on the Registers, but this was not published until many years after his death[1].

The French influence was slow in penetrating into Germany, where Papal documents had been for the most part left to antiquaries, who examined the leaden seals, and to lawyers, who looked on the subject as a branch of mainly obsolete jurisprudence. While an immense service was done to history by Philipp Jaffé, himself a Polish Jew, through the compilation of his great calendar of Papal documents down to 1198, his purpose was historical, not diplomatic. What he aimed at was to make as complete a list of the documents as was possible, in order to provide materials for the historian; and however meritorious as a pioneer, his work suffered from a neglect of the great French tradition. This was noted by Wilhelm Diekamp as the weak point not only of Jaffé but also of

---

[1] A German translation of it by S. Löwenfeld appeared in the Archivalische Zeitschrift, iii. (1878) 66–149.

his continuator Potthast[1]; and Heinrich Denifle made
the same criticism on Jaffé's editor, Kaltenbrunner[2]. But
at Vienna as early as 1854 the Institute for Austrian
Historical Research was established expressly on the
model of the École des Chartes at Paris[3], and Theodor
Sickel (afterwards Ritter von Sickel) came to take part
in its organization when he had spent five years in study
at the French capital and had become closely acquainted
with the work of the École[4]. It was in fact after completing a task of research entrusted to him by the French
Government that he entered upon his duties at the Vienna
Institute in 1856. Working thus on the method which he
brought with him, Sickel rose to be the second founder of
the study of diplomatic. In time he was made head of
the Institute, and when in 1881 it was resolved to erect
an Austrian Historical Institute at Rome he was appointed
its superintendent. By this means, though his own
special investigations had been devoted to Imperial
documents, he became the master spirit directing
an amount of energetic work upon the productions
of the Papal Chancery which was long unsurpassed in
Europe.

Meanwhile in the German Empire a movement was on
foot which had a profound influence on the study. The

[1] 'Sie übersahen gleichmässig die frühere Hauptarbeit über
ihren Gegenstand,...Potthast die Delisle's, Jaffé die der Bene-
dictiner': in Historisches Jahrbuch, iv. (1883), 217.

[2] Kaltenbrunner, he said, might have been saved from a
serious blunder, 'hätte er nicht die französischen Forscher so
vornehm ignoriert': Archiv für Literatur- und Kirchen-
Geschichte des Mittelalters, ii. (1886), 55.

[3] See E. von Ottenthal, in Mittheilungen des Instituts für
Österreichische Geschichtsforschung, xxix. (1908) 547.

[4] For the particulars of Sickel's biography, see *ibid.*
pp. 545–559.

greatest historical undertaking in that country, the Monumenta Germania Historica[1], was placed under the management of the Berlin Academy in 1872, and three years later its organization was reconstructed and the sphere of its operations extended. In 1876 it was determined to include the Letters of Gregory the Great; in 1880 and 1881 a selection of Papal Letters of the thirteenth century was arranged; a year later a proposal for the publication of all that remains of the Register of John VIII was adopted; and then by 1884 Theodor Mommsen had taken upon him to edit afresh the Liber Pontificalis[2], which was at that very time passing through the press under the masterly editorship of the Abbé (now Monsignor) Louis Duchesne.

This enlargement of the work of the Monumenta, side by side with the vigorous activity of the Institute at Vienna, soon established the German lands in the front rank in the special study of Papal diplomatic, which had previously been neglected there. The new enterprises involved preliminary researches, and just as for many years the Monumenta had had its missions in Italy for the discovery of materials for German history, so now the Academies of Vienna and Berlin and the committee

---

[1] It is interesting to recall that when the famous Baron vom Stein projected the foundation of the Monumenta Germaniae he was impressed by the fact 'that what had been done for Italy by Muratori and for France by the Congregation of St Maur had not yet been done for Germany.' In 1822 he invited Georg Heinrich Pertz, 'like another Muratori or Mabillon,' to take charge of the work. See Sir J. R. Seeley's Life and Times of Stein, iii. 440, 445, 1878. But Seeley comments with truth that a century earlier Leibnitz had planned a similar collection of historical materials.

[2] See the notices prefixed to the first, second, sixth, eighth, and ninth volumes of the Neues Archiv.

of the Monumenta vied with one another in the encouragement which they gave to the exploration of Papal documents. It was with the assistance of the Berlin Academy that Paul Ewald went to Italy in 1876, and this Academy also promoted Dr Julius von Pflugk-Harttung's researches in that country in 1882. The Vienna Academy sent Ferdinand Kaltenbrunner to Rome in 1878, and it was on behalf of the Monumenta that Samuel Löwenfeld made investigations in Papal documents at Paris. These examples illustrate the energy with which the new lines of study were pursued and the hearty support which the students received from public bodies.

The great advantages which thus enured to learning were due not only to the fresh stimulus given to Papal diplomatic but to the fact that the German and Austrian scholars brought to its criticism a long experience and an unsurpassed equipment in the analytical work which they or their teachers had done in connexion with the Monumenta and with the exploration of Imperial documents. On the one hand, there was the laborious collation of manuscripts and tracing of their affinities; on the other, the palaeographical examination of originals, the comparison of handwritings, the penetration of the structure of documents, the analysis of formulae, the establishment of Chancery rules. These principles of study were transplanted into a new field, and their results, if at times impaired by excess of refinement and an undue striving after originality, have in the past thirty years proved of remarkable value and importance.

Of the brilliant band of scholars who first entered the field two of the ablest were cut off before they had shown all the distinguished powers which they possessed: Ewald

died at 36, Diekamp at 31. Those who have since carried
on the work with eminent success need not be here mentioned by name; almost every page of my book bears
testimony to my indebtedness to them. But to one
scholar above all, Dr Harry Bresslau, it is right that
I should express my special obligations. His masterly
Handbuch der Urkundenlehre für Deutschland und Italien
is not only a marvellously complete guide to the immense
literature which has accumulated, very largely in scattered
monographs, on the subject of Papal documents; but it
stands alone in the comprehensiveness and lucidity of its
treatment. The author is not overweighted by his great
learning; and his sound judgement, his penetration into
the legal meaning of forms, and his acute criticism make
his book absolutely indispensable. Except in my fourth
and seventh chapters, I have made use of it at every
step, and though I have not always been able to accept
Dr Bresslau's conclusions I am certain that to him, more
than to any other living man, my book owes whatever
merit it may possess. Nor should I omit to acknowledge
my debt to Dr Paul Kehr for the assistance which I owe
to his works in attempting to disentangle the complex
and obscure changes in the organization of the Chancery
in the eleventh century. The chapter in which I discuss
them is probably the least satisfactory in my book, but
it would have been far darker without the light thrown
upon the subject by Dr Kehr.

In bringing to a close a work which, though small in
dimensions, is the outcome of protracted toil, it is a
pleasant duty to express my hearty thanks to the Master
and Fellows of Trinity College not only for the honour

they did me in electing me to the Birkbeck Lectureship but also in particular for the constant kindness which they showed me during the time when I enjoyed the privilege for a brief space of being accounted a member of their illustrious Society.

REGINALD L. POOLE.

26 *July* 1915.

LIST OF SOME ABBREVIATED REFERENCES

Acta.   Acta Pontificum Romanorum inedita, ed. by
                 J. von Pflugk-Harttung, 3 volumes, 1881–1886.

Bresslau.   Handbuch der Urkundenlehre für Deutschland
                 und Italien, vol. i. 2nd ed. 1912. This com-
                 prises only nine out of the nineteen chapters
                 of the first edition of 1889: when these latter
                 are cited, the edition is specified.

Greg. VII Reg.   Registrum, in Jaffé's Monumenta Gregoriana,
                 1865.

Gregorovius.   History of the City of Rome in the Middle Ages,
                 transl. by Mrs Hamilton, 1894–1902.

Inn. III Reg.   Regesta, in Migne, ccxiv.–ccxvi.

Jaffé, Reg.   Regesta Pontificum Romanorum, 2nd ed., 1881–
                 1888 (cited by the number of the document,
                 except where the volume is specified).

Mansi.   Conciliorum nova et amplissima Collectio.

Migne.   Patrologiae Cursus completus, Series Latina.

Mittheilungen.   Mittheilungen des Instituts für Österreichische
                 Geschichtsforschung.

Neues Archiv.   Neues Archiv der Gesellschaft für ältere Deutsche
                 Geschichtskunde.

Spec.   Specimina selecta Chartarum Pontificum Roma-
                 norum, ed. by J. von Pflugk-Harttung, 1885–
                 1887.

CONTENTS

I.

When we consider the forces which influenced mankind during the middle ages, it is evident that none can be compared with the Papacy in the continuous and decisive manner in which it penetrated every country of Western Europe, intervened in the affairs of church, and monastery, and town, even of kingdom and empire, and acted as mediator, as arbitrator, as judge. This influence was exerted in part by means of living agents, and when the system of appointing Legates was established much of the more important policy of the Popes was confided to them. But this was only a fraction of the work they did. Their daily business was conducted by letter; and it is the Papal Letters—or, as we commonly call them, Bulls—which formed the instrument by which the Papal authority was exercised. The letters being of such importance, it was necessary that they should be drawn up with care; and thus a staff of officers had to be employed as the Pope's secretaries. An organization already existing was adapted for this purpose, and its rules for carrying on its business became gradually more and more precise. When in the eleventh century the Pope sought to operate in a more extended sphere than he had previously been wont to do, it was the more needful to

safeguard the authenticity of his letters, not merely
by formal regularity but also by a variety of
patent marks of genuineness. Certain types were
elaborated which in the twelfth and thirteenth
centuries acquired a perfection of style and of
calligraphy which has never been surpassed. The
purpose of my present undertaking is to examine
the machinery by which the Pope's business was
done and the work which that machinery produced:
in other words, to trace the history of the Papal
Chancery and to describe the documents written
in it, the manner in which these documents were
drawn up, the persons through whose hands they
passed, and the processes which they underwent
before they were finally issued.

To speak of the Roman Chancery in the early
ages of the Papacy is indeed an anachronism, for
there could be no Chancery under that name
until the title of Chancellor was imported from the
Imperial system in the eleventh century. But
the anachronism is convenient, because the word
Chancery denotes exactly what we want to express,
the machinery by means of which the Pope conducted his business, his secretarial office. It
enables us to detach this limited field of study,
which is but a small and circumscribed department of the constitutional history of the Roman
Church, from the larger concerns in which the
history of the Papacy is involved. It is only
incidentally that we must notice the local conditions which explain the origin of some elements
in the Pope's staff of officers.

The subject is dry and technical; it has not

even the merit of introducing controversial topics. But it presents several features of interest. It illustrates in an unexpected way the relations of the Popes towards the City of Rome and towards other external forces with which they were brought into contact. It throws light on palaeography. It will show us how the old Roman school of penmen was superseded when the Pope ceased to look upon Rome as his habitual residence, and how a new style of writing was imported from the reformed models of the Carolingian Empire. There is also a literary interest, and this is a discovery of the last thirty years which has only been fully explained quite recently: namely the establishment of the rules of balance and cadence in the period, which form what is known as the Cursus Curiae Romanae. These rules were settled in the eleventh century, and they soon became a distinguishing mark of documents proceeding from the Papal Chancery. Indeed the beauty and delicate euphony of the sentences thus produced led in time to the adoption of the Cursus by the other Chanceries of Western Europe, and it persisted, though with abating purity, until the revival of classical learning in the fifteenth century. It is, however, one of the most remarkable points in the critical work which has gone on in the past generation, that the invention of the Cursus in the eleventh century was in fact a revival on somewhat different lines—an adaptation to a changed mode of accentuation—of a system of rhetoric which had prevailed in the ancient world down to the early part of the sixth century and

1—2

which can be traced in principle back to the
Athenian orators.

These are incidents in our enquiry, which only
claim mention now in order to show that even a
narrow subject ramifies into regions of a less
confined interest.

The materials for our study are primarily
the letters of the Popes themselves. These fall
naturally in point of time into two great periods.
In the former of these no documents remain
except in transcripts; in the latter we begin to
have to do with originals, at first very few in
number, but gradually and soon rapidly increasing.
The line of division is marked by the pontificate of
Hadrian I, which began two years before Charles
the Great became king of the Lombards. The
date is therefore a convenient one, because it
coincides with the introduction of a new factor
into Italian politics, which had a profound influence
upon the institutions of Rome. For the time
preceding Hadrian I the letters are preserved,
in copies of varying trustworthiness, in volumes
chiefly compiled, as we shall see, in the interest
of the definition of law. Some light is thrown on
the official conditions under which the Pope's
correspondence and other business were carried on
by the early evidence presented in the Liber
Pontificalis or collection of Lives of the Popes,
and in the Liber Diurnus, or book of forms in
use in the Chancery.

For the purposes of our present study it would
be out of place to explore the intricate questions

connected with the composition and structure of
the Liber Pontificalis [1]. It must suffice to say
that it includes elements which in their present
form go back at least as far as the early part of the
fourth century. The Catalogue of Popes known
as the Liberian, because it was revised during
the pontificate of Liberius (352–366), is in fact
an emended edition of a list drawn up in 336.
Another record incorporated in the Liber Pontificalis ends with the death of Felix IV (530);
this is distinguished as the Catalogus Felicianus:
whether it is an abridgement of an older and larger
book, a first edition of the complete work, or
whether it is the nucleus out of which that work
grew, need not be here considered. That the
book existed in its developed form before the end
of the seventh century is disputed by no one.
Thenceforward it was revised and continued, and
a second recension was made after the death of
Pope Cono (687), about which time an abridgement ending with this Pope is also preserved,
and is known as the Cononian Epitome. Continuators carry on the main work down to the
eighth and then the ninth century; but after 872
their notices are, for the most part, brief and it
is not until the accession of Gregory VII in 1073
that the Lives resume a character of contemporary
or nearly contemporary authority and often of
important value.

---

[1] Something on the subject will be found in Appendix I. My
references to the Liber Pontificalis are taken from the edition of
Monsignor Duchesne (1886–1892), except when that of Theodor
Mommsen (1898) is expressly cited.

The Liber Diurnus is in substance a manual for use in the Papal court. It contains a collection of formulae for the production of documents and of rules for the performance of official acts, and it assumed more or less its present shape between 685 and 751, though some parts may be a little earlier[1]. But the three manuscripts in which it is preserved differ in their arrangement and in the number of the documents which they contain, and a definitive text of the work has not yet been published[2]. The book was used in the Papal Chancery down to the eleventh century. Traces of it can be noticed under Alexander II, but it passed out of currency in the time of Gregory VII[3].

When about the beginning of the third century

[1] In the Vatican manuscript, formulae 1–63 represent a collection of the seventh century, probably made up out of more than one smaller collection already existing; formulae 64–81 are a continuation down to about 700; formulae 82–99 were put together under Hadrian I. A few additional formulae, found only in the Clermont manuscript, were supplied not long after 800.

[2] The last edition was made in 1889 by Theodor von Sickel from a manuscript in the Vatican archives which he believed to be older than 795, but which on palaeographical grounds I should place nearer the second quarter of the ninth century; and from the Clermont manuscript, now at Paris, which is assigned also to the ninth century. He was, however, not aware of the existence of a Bobbio manuscript, now at Milan, of which the text has long been expected at the hands of Monsignor Ratti. I should add that, while Sickel has greatly advanced the critical study of the text of the book—specially in his Prolegomena, published in the Sitzungsberichte of the Vienna Academy, cxviii. (1889), 7, 13—his edition has not at all superseded that which Rozière brought out some years earlier; for this contains a large body of notes which are of great value for the illustration of the subject-matter.

[3] Bresslau, Handbuch der Urkundenlehre für Deutschland und Italien, i. (1st ed., 1889), 623.

the Roman Church acquired the position of a corporate body capable of holding property, it was organized as a *collegium*, and for the conduct of its temporal business it required the employment of clerks or *notarii*[1]. These notaries were distributed among the regions of Rome. The Liber Pontificalis carries back this distribution to the first age of Christianity, and says that the city was divided by St Clement into seven regions, each of them provided with a notary for the purpose of recording the acts of martyrs in his region[2]. It is not necessary here to discuss this tradition, but it is quite possible that the division into seven regions may be traced as early as the pontificate of Fabian, who died in the year 250, for the primitive catalogue which was made use of in the compilation of the Liber Pontificalis contains the definite statement that this Pope 'divided the regions among deacons[3].' Too much stress need not be laid on the precise date, but it is unquestioned that at an early time the city of Rome was divided for ecclesiastical purposes into seven regions.

We have then to enquire what relation these

---

[1] Cf. K. J. Neumann, Der Römische Staat und die allgemeine Kirche, 1890, i. 102–110.

[2] 'Hic fecit VII regiones et dividit [*v.l.* divisit] notariis fidelibus ecclesiae qui gesta martyrum sollicite et curiose unusquisque per regionem suam diligenter perquireret': Lib. Pontif. i. 52, from the text known as the Felician Catalogue. The words 'fecit VII regiones' are not found in the later text called Cononian: *ibid.* (p. 231, Mommsen).

[3] 'Hic regiones divisit diaconibus,' in the Liberian Catalogue, Lib. Pontif. i. 4; Chron. min., ed. Mommsen (Monum. Germ. hist.), i. (1892). 75.

seven regions bore to the fourteen in which the
city was organized by Augustus[1]. One would
naturally assume that the seven ecclesiastical
regions were formed by grouping the civil regions
in pairs; but when we have definite testimony
to the existence of particular ecclesiastical regions,
they are not found to correspond in boundary
with the civil areas[2]. The truth appears to be
that the two systems were formed for different
purposes; and when the object for which the
ecclesiastical regions were established is understood,
it will be found that their arrangement throws
valuable light on the distribution of the Christian
population.

The civil regions were arranged on a principle
which presupposed that the inhabitants occupied
the heart of the city. No less than five of the
fourteen actually converged on the same point, the
meta sudans between the Forum and the Colosseum.
From that point the ist, iind, iiird, ivth, and xth
regions radiated. These comprised the central
and eastern parts of the city. The vith, viith,
and viiith made up the north; and the outlying
districts, running to the limits afterwards enclosed
by the walls of Aurelian (A.D. 272) on the east and
north-west, formed the vth and ixth. The extreme
south was divided among the xith, xiith, and
xiiith regions, and the district beyond the Tiber
made up the xivth. Except in the two instances

---

[1] The arrangement of the seven regions has been greatly
modified by recent researches. I follow the maps given in the
second edition of Formae Urbis Romae antiquae by H. Kiepert
and C. Huelsen, 1912, plate iii. Compare below, Appendix ii.

[2] See Duchesne's remarks, Lib. Pontif. i. 148, note 3.

where the numeration was interrupted so as to bring in outlying districts, it proceeded regularly, from south to east, north, and west.

Now when the Popes came to make provision for their dependants, they had to deal with a population small in number and limited in distribution. They did not need more than half the number of the civil regions, and the central districts hardly concerned them at all. The Christians were scattered in the poor and partly waste parts adjacent to the walls, and hence it was from the walls and not from the centre that their regions were constructed. The system of numbering from the south and following the walls up the east and then north and west was adopted on the analogy of the civil regions. Six ecclesiastical regions covered the space of thirteen civil ones; and the seventh, like the xivth civil region, was constituted by the district beyond the Tiber. But any attempt to co-ordinate the boundaries of the one system with the other leads to no result. There was no reason why the two should coincide, for they were formed with entirely different objects. The civil regions were arranged for the purpose of municipal administration; the ecclesiastical regions for the charitable service of a particular class of the inhabitants, a poor community which gathered most at the extremities of the city. They could not afford to live in the central districts, where moreover their society would probably not have been welcome.

The conclusion to which we are led by topographical considerations receives remarkable

support from the recorded traditions as to the dates
of the foundation of churches. Not indeed that
these traditions, so far at least as they concern the
first three centuries, can be accepted as relating
historical facts: there was always a natural tendency to attribute to foundations of all sorts an
antiquity beyond their due. But a tradition was
not likely to place the earliest churches in districts
which were altogether improbable, and from this
point of view its evidence is of value. Now the
church of St Pudentiana on the Viminal is traced
back to the middle of the second century[1]; in the
third we have mention of a church beyond the
Tiber, no doubt, that of St Mary[2]; and another,
that of St Cecilia, in the same region emerges in
the fourth[3]: on the Aventine, tradition speaks
of at least one church, that of St Prisca[4]. Of
the seven churches ascribed to the Emperor
Constantine, four, St Peter, St Paul, St Agnes, and
St Lawrence, stood outside the walls; and the
other three, the churches known later as St John
Lateran and St Cross in Jerusalem, and that of
SS. Marcellinus and Peter, were near together in
the extreme south-east of Rome[5]. There is no
sign of any Christian foundations in the districts
where the ancient population chiefly congregated.

The first exception to this rule appears in

[1] In a passage inserted in the life of Pius I, Lib. Pontif. XI.,
vol. i. 132, and note 8.

[2] *Ibid.* XVII., vol. i. 141 and note 5.

[3] See an inscription assigned to this century by G. B. de Rossi,
Inscript. Christ. Urbis Romae, i. 359 f.

[4] Gregorovius, i. 87, Duchesne, in Lib. Pontif. i. 517, note 45.

[5] Lib. Pontif. XXXIV., vol. i. 172, 176, 178–182.

a notice relating to the second quarter of the fourth century, when the church of St Mark is said to have been founded on the north-west of the Capitol; but this church is not historically attested until 499[1]. The Basilica of Liberius on the Esquiline, afterwards known as the Greater church of St Mary, is said to have been erected about 352[2]; the neighbouring church of St Praxedis, and the church on the south-west slope of the Palatine which acquired the name of St Anastasia, are attributed to the latter years of the fifth century; and in 527 a pagan edifice actually adjacent to the Forum was converted into the church of SS. Cosmas and Damian. But it was not until after the Byzantine conquest of the middle of the sixth century that derelict pagan buildings became generally available for Christian use[3]; and when the *diaconiae* were established nearly half of them were in districts where Christians had previously been strangers, in the ivth, viiith, xth, and xith civil regions:

[1] Lib. Pontif. xxxv., vol. i. 202 and note 5.

[2] *Ibid.* xxxvii. 8 (vol. i. 208). The dedication to St Mary was made by Xystus III. Dr J. P. Richter and Miss A. Cameron Taylor, in their work entitled The Golden Age of Classic Christian Art (1904), propose to carry back the mosaics in this church to a much earlier date than that of Liberius; but it may be doubted whether any of them are as old as his time.

[3] See G. McN. Rushforth, The Church of St Maria Antiqua, in Papers of the British School at Rome, i. (1902), 4 ff. This church which was discovered beneath that of S. Maria Liberatrice in 1900 is believed by the Rev. H. M. Bannister to go back 'to at least the first half of the fifth century' (English Historical Review, xviii., 1903, 338 ff.); but this argument rests upon a questionable interpretation of the attribute *antiqua*. Cf. W. de Grüneisen, Sainte Marie Antique, pp. 449 ff., 1911.

not one was in the district beyond Tiber[1]. The centre of the city was now open to Christians.

We have seen that the Liber Pontificalis contains an unhistorical tradition that St Clement divided the city into regions under seven notaries who were to record the acts of martyrs. In the notice of Fabian, who was Pope from 236 to 250, we have a somewhat different account. Here it is said that Fabian divided the regions among the deacons, and appointed seven subdeacons to have charge over the seven notaries, *qui septem notariis imminerent,* in order that they might faithfully collect the acts of martyrs[2]. Monsignor Duchesne sees here a distinction between rank in the church and rank at the Papal court: in the one the subdeacons by virtue of their orders had precedence, in the other the notaries[3]. It should be noticed, however, that while the passage as a whole is transcribed from the Catalogus Liberianus[4], a work of the middle of the fourth century, the sentence about the subdeacons is an insertion: all the Catalogus says is that Pope Fabian divided the regions among the deacons. Under Fabian's successor Cornelius there is documentary evidence that seven deacons and seven subdeacons were

[1] Duchesne, in Mélanges d'Archéologie et d'Histoire, vii. (1887), 238 f.

[2] 'Hic regiones dividit [*v.l.* divisit] diaconibus et fecit vii subdiaconos qui septem notariis imminerent ut gesta martyrum fideliter colligerent,' in the Felician Catalogue, Lib. Pontif. xxi., vol. i. 64, 148 and note 4 (pp. 238 and 27, ed. Mommsen).

[3] Cf. Greg. Magn. Reg. viii. 16, ed. L. M. Hartmann, 1893; cited below, p. 13, note 2.

[4] Lib. Pontif. i. 4.

already in existence[1], and there is no reason for doubting that they were attached to the regions.

After the time of Constantine the notaries of the holy Roman Church are sufficiently attested. They formed a Schola or guild, just as the notaries did at the imperial court. Our best evidence for this comes from a letter of Gregory the Great, in which the Schola of the seven Notarii of the regions is mentioned as corresponding in number to the subdeacons and the Defensores or guardians[2]. But members of the Schola are found much earlier than Gregory's time. The chief officer was the Primicerius notariorum[3]. According to some manuscripts, Laurentius, to whom St Augustine dedicated his Enchiridion was Primicerius of the Roman Church. Next to him was the Secundicerius, who is found attending the Constantinopolitan Council of 536[4]. It is not clear whether these two were then reckoned with the regionary notaries or ranked above and outside their number.

[1] Cornelii Epist. IX., in P. Coustant's Epistolae Romanorum Pontificum, i. (1721), 149 [Jaffé, Reg. 106]. Seven deacons were present at the Roman synod of 499: A. Thiel, Epistolae Romanorum Pontificum genuinae, i. 642 (1868).

[2] 'Quia igitur defensorum officium in causis ecclesiae et obsequiis noscitur laborare pontificum, hac eos concessa prospeximus recompensationis praerogativa gaudere, constituentes ut, sicut in schola notariorum et subdiaconorum per indultam longe retro pontificum largitatem sunt regionarii constituti, ita quoque in defensoribus septem, qui ostensa suae experientiae utilitate placuerint, honore regionario decorentur': Reg. VIII. 16.

[3] The same officer appears at Alexandria in 431, at Constantinople in 451, at Ravenna, and elsewhere: see the references in Bresslau, i. 194, note 2.

[4] 'Mennas venerabilis lector apostolicae sedis antiquae Romae et secundicerius notariorum': Mansi, Conciliorum nova et ampliss. Collect. viii. (1762), 896.

The Papal notaries had a place in the Pope's council analogous to that held by the Imperial notaries in that of the Emperor. Their forms of procedure resemble those of the officials of the civil government, especially of the senate. When necessary several of the notaries attended a synod; for instance, at the Lateran council of 649 the Primicerius notariorum and four regionary notaries were present[1]. They wrote the minutes of the proceedings and had charge of the official preparation of the Acts: in a word, they formed a secretary's office[2]. Such an office necessarily had records to keep, and the Papal archives can be traced back to a very early date[3]. Damasus I (366–384) built a 'new house' for them beside the church of St Lawrence in Prasina, known later as St Lawrence in Damaso[4]; from which fact it may be gathered that the collection was of old standing. How long it continued at St Lawrence's is unknown; but it had evidently been removed to the Lateran by 649[5]. The archives and the library were, and had long been, kept together, and they were under the charge of the Primicerius

[1] Mansi, x. 891, 903, 926, 930.

[2] As late as the fifteenth century the Papal protonotaries, who took the place of the regionary notaries, retained the right of making the minutes at consistories and of preparing their decrees: see Bresslau, i. 195.

[3] See *ibid.* pp. 149 ff.

[4] 'Archibis fateor volui nova condere tecta,
  Addere praeterea dextra laevaque columnas,
  Quae Damasi teneant proprium per saecula nomen':
De Rossi, Inscriptiones Christianae Urbis Romae, ii. 151.

[5] There are a number of references to documents in the Scrinium in the Acts of the Lateran council of this year: Mansi, x. 863 ff. (*e.g.* 911, 914, 923).

notariorum[1].   Besides the archives of the Lateran
there was a special depository of documents in the
Confessio sancti Petri in the crypt of the great
Basilica across the Tiber; but whether they were
permanently preserved there, or whether, as space
was wanted, they were transferred to the Lateran
or to the muniments of the chapter of St Peter's,
remains obscure[2].

The Primicerius notariorum was one of the
most influential members of the Papal court.
He together with the archpriest and the archdeacon
'kept the place of the holy apostolic see' during
a vacancy[3]: as we should say, they were the
guardians of the spiritualities.   The Primicerius
was also important as a counsellor of the Pope.
Just as in the parallel case of the Imperial notaries,
his business training and experience qualified
him for employment on diplomatic missions and
in weighty matters of administration.   But his
primary duty was to take charge of the Papal
archives; it was he who saw to the drawing up
and despatching of the Pope's correspondence.

The actual writing of the Pope's letters was
performed by the notaries, who as members of the
Chancery (to anticipate the use of this word) are
called Scriniarii.   It has been maintained that the
two offices of notary and Scriniarius were distinct;
that the one wrote the documents and the other
kept the records.   Now there is no doubt that
scrinium may denote the archives, and there are

[1] Bresslau, i. 152.
[2] *Ibid.* p. 154.
[3] Liber Diurnus, nn. 59, 61–63, ed. Sickel.

texts which mention Scriniarii as having charge of the archives[1]. But at the same time it is certain that the Primicerius notariorum was the chief keeper of the archives, and there is no sufficient reason for doubting that the notaries under him were employed in a double capacity. The combined title, Notarius et Scriniarius appears in the Liber Diurnus[2], and becomes quite usual from the time of Hadrian I in the latter part of the eighth century[3]. It is perhaps needless to insist further on this identity of office, because in Imperial inscriptions and in the Notitia Dignitatum the Scriniarii are secretaries or clerks of account[4]. In a law of Justinian the words Scrinium and Schola are used, almost if not quite alternatively, to denote all sorts of offices under the Praefectus praetorio Africae[5]. In this as in other ways the Papal administration modelled itself closely on the system of the Empire.

Thus the Scrinium was the office of the notaries, the Chancery; and it was this at least as early as the time of Gregory the Great. The notaries were Scriniarii, and might be called equally by the double title and by either of the two separately.

---

[1] Liber Diurnus, n. 33.

[2] n. 103, 104.

[3] A century later the word Scriniarii by itself is used to designate the persons whose business it was to draw up documents for the Pope. Thus Nicholas I, *a.* 865 writes: 'Hanc autem epistolam ideo more solito scribi non fecimus, quia et legatus vester sustinere non potuit et ob festa Paschalia scriniarios nostros, eo quod debitis vacabant occupationibus, habere ut debuimus non voluimus': Monum. Germ., Epist. vi. 312 [Jaffé, Reg. 2788].

[4] Bresslau, i. 197, note 2.

[5] i Cod. xxvii. i.

It may be added that Scriniarii, so designated, are not peculiar to Rome: they are found at Terracina, Ravenna, Milan, Grado, and even outside Italy at Mainz[1]. At Rome the office was a Schola or guild which supplied a professional career. Young men entered it to obtain a training. They received the tonsure or minor orders; even the Primicerius and Secundicerius were sometimes married men. The offices appear to have gained an hereditary character and to have been filled mainly by members of the nobility of the city. The number of Scriniarii appointed in early times is not known: to judge from later times there may have been about a dozen[2].

Below the Primicerius and the Secundicerius ranked the Arcarius. He was the keeper of the chest, in early times a person of subordinate rank, but holding an office which gradually rose in importance: he became the Pope's treasurer[3]. He is first found mentioned in an inscription in St Paul's without the Walls assigned to the sixth century[4]. Towards the end of the seventh it is noted as unusual that Pope Agatho left the office for a time unfilled, or, as his biographer puts it,

[1] Bresslau, i. 197, note 4.

[2] At the Roman synod of 963 there appear certainly thirteen; see Liudprand, Hist. Ottonis, IX.: but some of them may have been town notaries not immediately attached to the Papal court.

[3] In the ninth century we find the post held by bishops; but in the tenth several Arcarii were married men.

[4] Pierluigi Galletta, Del Primicero della santa Sede apostolica e di altri Uffiziali maggiori del sacro Palagio Lateranense (1776), pp. 108 f.; G. B. de Rossi, Roma sotteranea, iii. (1877), 521.

was himself made Arcarius, and did the work of the Arcaria—the word appears in some manuscripts as Arcariva—personally[1]. There is no evidence to show that the Arcarius had anything to do with the notariate. The Saccellarius was apparently introduced on the reconquest of Italy by Justinian, but he is not definitely found until the end of the seventh century. He was the Pope's paymaster. He was often a regionary notary; sometimes he was also librarian: his connexion with the treasury might be not unnaturally associated with the charge of the library. Indeed, the first time we find a Saccellarius and a Bibliothecarius mentioned by name in the Liber Pontificalis, the two offices were held by the same person, the future Pope Gregory II[2].

The Primus Defensorum or Primicerius Defensorum dates apparently from Gregory the Great, when he established in 598 the seven Priores in the Schola Defensorum as regionary officers. There is no evidence that he was a notary; but since the duties of a Defensor were not limited to the guardianship of the poor, of widows and orphans, but extended over various fields of administration and jurisdiction[3], it is not improbable that he commonly was one.

[1] 'Hic ultra consuetudinem arcarius ecclesiae Romanae efficitur et per semetipsum causa [*v.l.* causam] arcarivae [*v.l.* arcariae] disposuit, emittens videlicet desuscepta per nomencolatorem manu sua obumbratas': Lib. Pontif. LXXXI. 17, vol. i. 350.

[2] 'Subdiaconus atque sacellarius factus, bibliothecae illi est cura commissa': *ibid.* XCI., vol. i. 396 (in the longer recension).

[3] See P. Hinschius, Kirchenrecht, i. (1869) 377, and the references to the Register of Gregory the Great there given.

The Nomenculator represents a well-known servant in the domestic establishments of ancient Rome; but he had risen from a servile position to a place of honour[1]. He is first mentioned at the Papal court under Pope Agatho (678–681)[2]; then he appears in 710, when he accompanied Pope Constantine with three other officers of the Chancery on his visit to Constantinople[3]. His functions are not clearly defined, but we gather that he and the Saccellarius received and dealt with petitioners who approached the Pope on processions[4]. In 745 we find Gregory Notarius regionarius et numenculator performing the old office of introducing envoys at a Roman synod[5].

These six offices all belonged to the clergy, though they were usually in minor orders. The Protoscriniarius, who has been often considered to belong to the college of notaries, does not appear until later: he was not a member of the college and he might be a layman. But I defer giving any account of him, because it is in several ways convenient to break off the history of the early organization of the Papal Chancery at the pontificate of Hadrian I. One reason is that in his

[1] The origin of the name was in time forgotten, and it became Amminiculator or the like: Liudprand, Hist. Ottonis, IX., and below, p. 51.

[2] Above, p. 18, note 1.

[3] Lib. Pontif. XC. 3, vol. i. 389.

[4] Another account says that he took charge of widows and orphans, the prisoners and the oppressed; but this comes from the Ottonian Notitia (concerning which see below, Appendix IV). This special duty belonged to the Defensores.

[5] Bonifatii Epist. L., ed. Jaffé (or LIX., ed. Dümmler), in three places.

tenth year he introduced more than one important new feature into the form of his documents. It was in the course of that year, at Easter, 15 April 781, that Charles the Great paid his first visit to Rome[1] and advanced by a further stage the establishment of the Papal States which had been begun by his father Pippin[2]. Very soon we find that Hadrian adopted the Frankish practice of using a double form of dating his documents: the Scriptum gave the name of the notary who wrote the text; and the Data (afterwards Datum) bore the name of the officer who completed and authenticated it[3]. He also omitted the regnal year of the Emperor at Constantinople and substituted his own pontifical year[4]. Thirdly, he adopted the rule, except in letters addressed to sovereigns, of placing his name first in the title or superscription of the document.

Another reason for making a division at this point is the accident that no original document is preserved until his time[5]. For the centuries before Hadrian I we have to rely entirely upon transcripts, and these transcripts fail to give us

[1] Ann. Regni Franc. *s.a.* (p. 56, ed. F. Kurze, 1895).

[2] Cf. G. Richter, Annalen der Deutschen Geschichte, ii. (1885), 687; Codex Carolinus, Epist. LXX.

[3] Cf. Specimina, 9.

[4] These two innovations are first found in a document of 1 December 781 printed by Baluze, Miscell., ed. Mansi, iii. 3 *b* 1762 [Jaffé, Reg. 2435.]. Hadrian's earlier form of dating may be found in a Bull of 20 February 772 transcribed in the Farfa Chartulary (Il Regesto di Farfa, ed. I. Giorgi and U. Balzani, ii., 1878, 83 ff. [Jaffé, Reg. 2395]).

[5] The supposed fragments of Bulls of John V and Sergius I are Dijon forgeries of the eleventh century. See Appendix III.

an exact representation of the original. Most
commonly they were copied out and preserved on
account of their legal value, as they conferred
privileges or gave decisions on disputed matters.
The number of these is large, more than 2500, but
few of them belong to a date at all near the original
time of writing. There are not, therefore, only the
elements of uncertainty or of corruption which
usually appear in copies; but the reasons which
caused the copies to be made rendered it natural
that the originals should not be transcribed in
their entirety. The formal beginnings and endings
of the documents—what are technically known
as the protocols—are abbreviated or altogether
omitted; and in this process the date of issue is
most commonly left out. It is impossible, therefore, to treat these transcripts with the same
critical rules which we can apply to originals; but
the general features of the documents are un-
mistakeable.

In the first place it is manifest that they
carried on the forms used by the Roman Emperors
and their officials; in other words, they are drawn
up in the form of Letters. Of course, I am
speaking of the mass of Papal documents to which
we are accustomed to give the name of Bulls. A
far more limited series, consisting of Acts of
Councils and judicial Sentences to which the Pope
was a party, has a different structure and does not
enter into our present consideration. Bulls from
first to last are drawn up as Letters, in principle
on the same model as the letters of Cicero. In
examining the structure of these letters we have to

distinguish the material part, or Text, from the formal Protocols which precede and follow it. The Text contains the information or the decision which the writer desires to communicate, and it necessarily allows him freer play for individualities of style and expression than do the Protocols, although even in the Text there were rules of rhythm and accustomed formulae which were faithfully observed. The Protocols on the other hand are strictly bound to a model which permits little or no variation. The Pope announces his title and names the person whom he addresses, with or without a greeting. This is all put in the third person[1], whereas in the Text the writer speaks in the first and speaks to the person whom he addresses in the second[2]. The first person is used also in the Subscription.

The Pope might place his name before or after that of the person he addressed. At first the usage was unsettled, but from Leo the Great onwards most of the Popes preferred to put their names second, and this practice continued at least until the eighth century[3]. The Pope commonly designated himself *episcopus,* sometimes *episcopus catholicae ecclesiae* or *episcopus Romanae ecclesiae,* sometimes *papa*; but this last name passed out of use

----

[1] Occasionally, in the Address, the second person appears in the possessive pronoun, *e.g. tuis* in place of *suis*; and in the Greeting, the first person.

[2] This might be either in the singular or plural; by degrees the singular became the rule. Conversely in a letter addressed to the Pope he was invariably mentioned in the plural.

[3] Thus Pope Zachary, Monumenta Moguntina, n. LXVI. p. 184 (n. LXXX., in Monum. Germ., Epist. iii. 356) [Jaffé, Reg. 2286].

in the Superscription of documents and was only revived in a type of documents entirely distinct in form, the Brief, towards the close of the middle ages. From the end of the sixth century, the pontificate of Gregory the Great, the word *episcopus* was often followed by the words *servus servorum Dei*. This is occasionally found at an earlier date, but it did not become the rule until the ninth century. The Greeting is by no means regularly expressed, or at least not represented in the transcripts, during the earlier centuries. In the fourth century Liberius and Damasus I used *in Domino salutem*[1] or *in Domino aeternam salutem*[2]. The formula becomes more frequent from the pontificate of Adeodatus, who was elected in 672: he wrote, *Salutem a Deo et benedictionem nostram*. But the Greeting continued far from being a constant feature, and it seldom crystallized into *Salutem et apostolicam benedictionem* until the tenth century, and was not fixed until the eleventh[3]. In the more solemn form of document the place of the Greeting was taken by the emphatic words 'for ever,' *in perpetuum*.

When the material part—the Text—of the letter is concluded we reach the final Protocol, consisting of the Subscription and the Date. In early times the Pope did not sign his name. He wrote instead his Farewell: *Deus te incolumem custodiat*, or, in the accustomed form of the correspondence of the day, *Bene vale, frater carissime* or *Opto te, frater carissime, semper bene valere*[4].

---

[1] Coustant, i. 573 [Jaffé, Reg. 239].
[2] *Ibid.* 448 [Jaffé, Reg. 223].   [3] See Appendix III.
[4] These two forms alternate in the letters of St Cyprian and

From the end of the sixth century the Pope would not style a bishop *frater carissime*, but employed the more distant phrase *venerabilis frater*. To princes such a form as *Incolumem excellentiam tuam* (or *vestram*) *gratia superna custodiat* was appropriate, and to Emperors this was sometimes expressed in a more ample style. It should be noticed that the Farewell often occurs in the plural when the body of the letter is drawn up in the singular. The commonest form, which we find as early as the fourth century, was simply *Bene valete*. This became constant in the seventh or eighth century, and served in fact as the Pope's signature.

In earlier documents the Date has been omitted in the process of transcription. The great bulk of the documents of the first six centuries has been transmitted in collections of Decretals, and it was the legal decision, and not the precise date, which was of importance from the point of view of the compilers. Still dates are preserved in the Decretals of Siricius (384–398), and there we find them given by the names of the Consuls and by the day reckoned after the ancient Roman manner. Later, the regnal year of the Emperor was added, but not yet the year of the pontificate. The practice of authenticating Papal letters with a leaden seal or *bulla* can be traced from the middle of the sixth century. The seal bore only the Pope's name in the genitive, as LEONIS PAPAE,

---

Cornelius, Coustant, i. 125–144, 167–194. The latter is a translation of the Greek forms found *e.g.* in letters of Julius I to the clergy of Antioch and of Alexandria, Coustant, i. 388, 404 [Jaffé, Reg. 186, 188].

with a small Greek cross, and perhaps a star or another cross or a ☧ monogram[1]. The transferred application of the name Bull to the document itself was not established until late in the middle ages, and then it was chiefly employed to indicate a particular type of letter with which we are not at present concerned. The common use of the word in English is free from objection, so long as it is understood that it is a conventional use without early authority.

Before entering upon the subject of the manner in which Papal documents were officially recorded, I may say something as to the transmission of these older letters of which the originals no longer exist. At an early time selections were made of Papal letters which were deemed of special importance as defining points of law. Of these the most famous is the small series of Decreta or Decretales which were collected by Dionysius Exiguus in the first quarter of the sixth century, and are printed in the first volume of the Bibliotheca Iuris Canonici Veteris edited by Henry Justel or Justeau in 1661. They begin with Pope Siricius towards the end of the fourth century. This collection in an enlarged form became widely known in the West during the eighth and ninth centuries. It must of course be carefully distinguished from the Pseudo-Isidorian work which

---

[1] The apostles' heads came in later: that of St Peter was introduced in the time of Victor II, and those of St Peter and St Paul under Paschal II. By Innocent III the two heads were interpreted as indicating the authority of Rome over all churches: Reg. I. 235.

was compiled and largely forged about 847. The three books of the Pseudo-Isidorian Decretals contain in book i. sixty letters of Roman bishops from St Clement to the beginning of the fourth century, all of which are spurious. Book ii. contains other famous documents, such as the forged Donation of Constantine together with genuine Canons of Councils; and in book iii. there is a series of a hundred and twenty Decretals and other letters from Sylvester I to Gregory II (who died in 731), and of these more than a quarter are spurious[1]. Most of these were fabricated at one time for a definite political object, but some of them are traceable to an earlier date. In an uncritical age the Pseudo-Isidorian collection was soon accepted without question, though there are reasons for thinking that the Roman court was not so easily deceived as were the clergy of the church in Gaul. Still, before long it acquired an undisputed position, and was used, together with the genuine Decretals, as materials for selection and codification in such a way as to constitute one of the elements in the formation of the body of Canon Law.

Many other Papal letters exist in a variety of sources. Early in the eighteenth century Dom Coustant spent his life in collecting all he could find; but he issued no more than one folio volume of Epistolae Romanorum Pontificum,

---

[1] Decretales Pseudo-Isidoriani, ed. P. Hinschius, 1863; compare the elaborate article on the subject by E. Seckel in Herzog and Hauck's Realencyklopädie der protest. Theologie, xvi. (1905), 265–307.

extending down to the death of Leo the Great in 461. A similar fate befell his continuator, A. Thiel, nearly a century and a half later, whose single volume published in 1868 carries on the series from 461 to 523. After this date the letters of many Popes, so far as they are preserved, have been edited in several forms, some of them in the Collections of Councils. But no attempt on a large scale has been made to continue the series for the succeeding period. There is indeed a miscellaneous and ill-arranged collection of Papal letters which was published by Dr Julius von Pflugk-Harttung under the title of Acta Pontificum Romanorum Inedita in three volumes between 1880 and 1888; but the documents are not all in fact unpublished and they are not edited with sufficient care. In spite of its defects, however, it is the only single book easily accessible which provides a large collection of specimens extending from early times to 1198, and as such I shall constantly refer to it.

The lack of any complete collection of Papal letters after 523 has been to some extent made good by the calendars produced by Philipp Jaffé and August Potthast. The former scholar, with whom at the moment we are alone concerned, published in 1851 a chronological catalogue of the whole series of extant documents, so far as he could find them, down to 1198. In this Regesta Pontificum Romanorum he dealt in a masterly way with 11,171 Papal documents which he described in five years of arduous toil from some 1700 different volumes, and gave full references to the books in which they are to be found. A second edition prepared by Paul Ewald, Ferdinand Kaltenbrunner, and Samuel Löwenfeld, under the general supervision of Wilhelm Wattenbach appeared between 1881 and 1888. In this the number of documents was enormously increased and the total raised to 17,679. But the work had not long been completed before a proposal was set on foot by Professor Paul Kehr of Göttingen for the production of a new Regesta Romanorum Pontificum, and the amassing of materials has been going on for nearly twenty years past. But the plan of the catalogue is different from Jaffé's. Instead of arranging the documents under each Pope in order of time, Dr Kehr classifies them under the headings of the region and the person or institution to which they were addressed. Consequently, until the work is finished, its value will be appreciated principally by students of those regions and churches, rather than by students of the history of the Papacy; and not until the work is complete and fully indexed will it be permissible to remove Jaffé from the front rank of books of reference. At present five volumes dealing with Italy[1] have appeared; and a sixth, beginning a German series[2], has been edited in association with Kehr by Professor Albert Brackmann of Marburg.

The existence of this multitude of scattered

[1] Italia Pontificia: i. Roma (1906), ii. Latium (1907), iii. Etruria (1908), iv. Umbria, Picenum, Marsia (1909), v. Aemilia (1910).

[2] Germania Pontificia: i. Salzburg and Trent (1911).

letters leads us to the question in what form the Popes caused their documents to be preserved, in other words to be registered, at or about the time of their production. The practice of keeping transcripts of documents on rolls of papyrus is known to have prevailed among the officials of the Roman Empire. These Commentarii were the models on which the Papal Registers were based[1]; and in the beginning it was the rule to enter in such books not only the documents which issued from the office of the person to whom the Register belonged but also many of the documents which were received at that office. But no Papal Register of ancient date is known to be in existence. That of Gregory the Great is but a selection from his original Register, made several centuries later; and until recent years it was supposed that no Registers were made in the Papal Chancery until his time. The erroneousness of this opinion has been proved by an analysis of several compilations of Papal and other letters, and each of these in turn has carried back the system to an earlier date.

First, the examination of an important collection transcribed at the beginning of the twelfth century and known as the Collectio Britannica[2] made it certain that Gelasius I (492–496) had

---

[1] This was shown by Dr Bresslau, Die Commentarii der Römischen Kaiser und die Registerbücher der Päpste, in the Zeitschrift der Savigny-Stiftung für Rechtsgeschichte, vi. (1885), Roman. Abth. pp. 242–260; cf. R. von Heckel, Das päpstliche und Sicilische Registerwesen, in Archiv für Urkundenforschung, i. (1908), 394–424.

[2] Addit. MS 8873, in the British Museum.

a Register[1]. Then it was shown from the collection published by Quesnel[2] that a group of Decretals was available for reference as early as 443[3], and their transcription could hardly have been made from any but official Registers. Thirdly, a remarkable composite collection of documents derived from four different Registers, those of Ravenna, of the Roman Prefecture, of Carthage, and of the Roman Curia, and distinguished as the Collectio Avellana[4], furnishes evidence that Papal Registers existed not only under Zosimus (417–418) but even fifty years before him under Liberius (352–366)[5]. It may therefore be inferred that the adoption of the civil practice began almost coincidently with the new political powers which the Church acquired under Constantine.

Our knowledge of the fact that Registers were kept depends upon the accident that documents were transcribed from them for legal purposes, to define rules and lay down the canonical practice in doubtful matters. It would be impossible within my limits, even were the subject strictly relevant, to touch upon the considerable

[1] See Paul Ewald, Die Papstbriefe der Brittischen Sammlung, in Neues Archiv, v. (1880), 277–414, 505–596.

[2] App. ad Leonis Magni Opera, 1675; and in Migne, lvi.

[3] See Duchesne, La première Collection Romaine des Décrétales, in Atti del ii° Congresso de Archeologia Christiana, 1900 (Rome, 1902), pp. 159–162.

[4] The manuscript formerly at Fonte Avellana (Cod. Vatic. Lat. 4961) is now regarded as inferior to the Vatican Cod. Lat. 3787. See O. Günther, Epistulae Imperatorum Pontificum aliorum (Corp. Script. eccles. Lat. xxxv.), 1895, proleg. pp. xviii–xxiii.

[5] See Harold Steinacker's important paper Über das älteste päpstliche Registerwesen, in Mittheilungen, xxiii. (1902), 1–49.

critical apparatus which has been accumulated
in the past thirty years relative to the transmission
of Papal letters when the Registers are preserved
neither in the originals nor in copies; still less
would it be appropriate to enter into the discussion
of a number of intricate questions about which
controversy has arisen. To us the collections to
which I have referred are of immediate interest
only as furnishing evidence for the preservation
through many centuries of the actual Registers
of Papal documents which are now lost. Their
study for their own sake belongs not to the history
of the Chancery but to that of the sources of
Canon Law[1]. Still it may be here noticed that
one deduction can be drawn with reasonable
confidence from these materials, namely, that the
documents were entered in the Register as they
stood, without abbreviation of the Protocols or
of other formal parts[2]. The same fact has been
demonstrated from an examination of the Papal
letters quoted by the venerable Bede[3] from the
copies which Nothelm had made from the Registers
at Rome[3]. Hence from these transcripts we are
enabled partly to reconstruct the Registers from

[1] See Friedrich Maassen, Geschichte der Quellen und der
Literatur des canonischen Rechts im Abendlande, 1870.

[2] Steinacker, *ubi supra*, pp. 14, 36 ff.

[3] Mommsen, Die Papstbriefe bei Beda, in Neues Archiv, xvii.
(1892), 387–396. Bede indeed expressly says that Nothelm
'Romam veniens nonnullas ibi beati Gregorii papae simul et
aliorum pontificum epistulas, perscrutato eiusdem sanctae ecclesiae Romanae scrinio, permissu eius qui nunc ipsi ecclesiae praeest
Gregorii pontificis invenit, reversusque nobis nostrae historiae
inserendas...adtulit': Hist. eccl. Gent. Angl., praef., i. 6, ed.
C. Plummer, 1896.

which they are taken.   It may further be observed that the custom of registering documents received as well as documents despatched broke down in the course of the sixth century, and that thereafter documents received, together with miscellaneous minutes and memoranda, only appear by way of exception.

The Register of Gregory the Great cannot be reconstructed in its entirety.   We know that it existed in the ninth century: there were fourteen volumes on papyrus, one for each year of Gregory's pontificate, arranged by the Indictions.   But what we now possess is a series of some 850 letters preserved in three independent collections.   These cannot at all represent the entire number; indeed, at least 77 other letters have been found outside these collections: and it is evident that an average number of 66 letters a year must be only a small proportion of the documents actually despatched by the Pope.   It is almost certain that the transcripts preserved were taken directly from the original Register.   The entire text of the letters was inserted in the Register, and when in the transcripts the Protocols are abbreviated, this change is attributable to the copyists[1].   It may therefore be laid down that in Gregory's time the documents were still transcribed into the Register as they stood, without any omissions of substance, and that the shorter form in which some of them are now preserved is due to the desire of transcribers to retain all that was of material importance while sparing their labour by the omission

[1] Cf. Steinacker, *ubi supra*, pp. 8 ff., 41 f.

of details which did not affect the value of the document as a statement of law. It was sufficient for them that the Pope had laid down a particular rule or principle; it was indifferent at what date he laid it down or to whom he directed his letter. The documents were transcribed for legal, not historical purposes.

For the time following Gregory the Great it is possible to trace the continued existence of the Registers for nearly three hundred years, but in all cases but one the evidence is obtained from collections made for canonical purposes in the Hildebrandine age. The book compiled by Cardinal Deusdedit and the British Museum collection contain documents expressly stated to be taken from the Registers of Honorius I[1] in the seventh century, of Gregory II[2] and Gregory III[3] in the eighth, and of Leo IV[4], Nicholas I[5], John VIII[6], and Stephen V[7] (885–891) in the ninth. Only of John VIII do we possess a distinct Register comprising his last seven years, from 876 to 882, and containing 314 letters. This is preserved in a manuscript of the second half of the eleventh century, written in the hand characteristic of Monte

[1] Die Kanonessammlung des Kardinals Deusdedit, i. 235, 236, iii. 138, 139, ed. V. Wolf von Glanvell, 1905.

[2] *Ibid.* iii. 140, 141.

[3] *Ibid.* i. 237.

[4] Forty-five letters in the British Museum MS: see Ewald, *ubi supra*, pp. 376–396; Deusdedit, iii. 63.

[5] Ewald, p. 587, n. 54; Deusdedit, i. 259.

[6] Fifty-five letters, Ewald, pp. 295–320; Deusdedit; ii. 90.

[7] Otherwise Stephen VI. Thirty-one letters, Ewald, pp. 399–414; Deusdedit, i. 244, iv. 183.

Cassino[1]. It was formerly believed not to represent the actual Register but to consist of a selection of letters made from it in order to illustrate and define the Pope's political activity. This opinion has been disturbed by the proof that the scribe of the existing manuscript was a mere copyist without the capacity of making a selection himself. But it does not follow that the book from which he transcribed was not itself a selection from the original Register[2]. The circumstance that it only includes one single Privilege[3],—and that a document which reserved a particular lawsuit for the Pope's hearing, and was therefore of canonical importance,—seems to favour the conclusion that the older hypothesis was essentially correct[4]. An average of about one letter a week can manifestly not represent the Pope's complete correspondence. On the other hand it must be admitted that we know too little of the principles on which in the ninth century Registers were drawn up, and what sorts of documents were normally inserted in them, to be able to lay down with confidence that the collection of letters of John VIII is not his

[1] Cf. E. A. Loew, The Beneventan Script, 1914, p. 20. Apparently the second and third volumes of the Register were taken to Monte Cassino, and the first left at Rome. Hence the compiler of the Collectio Britannica was able to include only documents from 872 to 876. See Erich Caspar, Studien zum Register Johanns VIII, in Neues Archiv, xxxvi. (1911), 105 f.

[2] Dr Caspar contests this view, p. 103, principally on the ground that technical phrases used in Registers are reproduced in the book.

[3] N. 100, in Caspar's edition, Monum. Germ., Epist. vii. 93 (1912).

[4] Cf. Bresslau, i. 106 note 5, and 740.

actual Register. Still the examination of his book, which has been conducted with great thoroughness[1], has at least established that the system of registration which prevailed in the ninth century was less complete than had been observed in earlier times : the title and greeting were suppressed, and the address abbreviated[2]. It is also clear that the letters in the Register were transcribed not from the originals as prepared for dispatch, but from their draughts[3]. The chronological order of the documents was apt to be deranged when the Pope was on his travels; but even when he was in Rome an amount of irregularity is found which has led to the supposition that the dates were inserted by the author or the transcriber of the Register, or at least that when the draughts were undated the registrar automatically inserted the words *Data ut supra*, which have caused much perplexity to critics[4].

These questions have deserved mention, though their final solution is not perhaps yet decided, because the existence of so large a fragment of a ninth-century Register is a unique phenomenon,

[1] See A. Lapôtre, L'Europe et le Saint-Siège à l'Époque Carolingienne, i., Le Pape Jean VIII, 1895, pp. 1–29; and Caspar, in Neues Archiv, xxxvi. 77–156.

[2] Caspar, *ubi supra*, p. 107, and in Mittheilungen, xxxiii. (1912), 389.

[3] The appearance however of words like *igitur* in the opening clause of a document does not, as Caspar thinks (Neues Archiv, xxxvi. 124), necessarily involve the omission of an Arenga by the registrar : exactly the same use of *igitur* and similar particles may be found in Anglo-Saxon charters; *e.g.* Offa, 794, in Heming's Chartulary, p. 54, and Coenwulf, 814, in Facsimiles of Ancient Charters in the British Museum, ii. 14.

[4] See Caspar, pp. 127 ff.

and because, but for the scanty extracts from
the Register of Stephen V, no further trace is
known of any Papal Register having been kept
until the time of Alexander II[1] in the latter part
of the eleventh century. It has even been suggested that in this interval of Papal obscurity
no Registers were ever kept[2], and it is certainly
a remarkable coincidence that at the same point,
in the middle of the Life of Stephen V, the Liber
Pontificalis ceases abruptly in the middle of a
sentence[3]; but though this suggestion cannot be
excluded, it is more probable that the lack of evidence is due to the fact that the Registers contained
no documents which would be of service to the
compilers of the collections which with the one
exception mentioned supply the only proof that
documents continued to be registered after the
time of Gregory the Great.

[1] See below, p. 123, note 3.
[2] Lapôtre, p. 16.
[3] ii. 196, ed. Duchesne.

II.

The earliest papal document of which the
original is known to be preserved is a fragment
of a letter of Hadrian I of the year 788. For the
time before this nearly 2500[1] exist in transcripts;
but, apart from a large number of admitted
forgeries, they were so often abbreviated or modified in their formal parts that we cannot deduce
from them with confidence the exact shape which
the documents assumed under different Popes.
The second original preserved is a Privilege of
Paschal I of 819, but though the number of originals
gradually increases, the growth is slow until the
second quarter of the eleventh century, when
papyrus was superseded by parchment in the
Chancery of Benedict VIII (1020–1022)[2]. But
from the moment that our originals begin we are
enabled to analyse their forms and to trace the
changes which they underwent from time to time.
Still it is to be remembered that out of about
1600 Bulls in existence belonging to the period

---

[1] The second edition of Jaffé's Regesta enumerates 2461, but
that was published 33 years ago.

[2] Bresslau, i. 73. Parchment came into use some time earlier,
but the supposed earliest original written on it, John XVIII's bull
for Paderborn (1005, Spec. 10), has been shown by Paul Ewald, in
Neues Archiv, ix. (1884), 332 f., and Dr Bresslau, in Mittheilungen,
ix. (1888), 16–24, to be a facsimile copy.

from Hadrian I to Leo IX only some forty are preserved in originals.

Apart from the fact that originals now begin to be available for our study, the pontificate of Hadrian I is marked out as the proper date for beginning the Second Period of the history of the Chancery; not his accession to the Papacy, but his tenth year. In the course of that year, as we have seen, at Easter 781, Charles the Great was in Rome, and shortly afterwards Hadrian abandoned the practice of dating his documents by the regnal years of the Emperor in the East. The mention of the Imperial year with the Consular year and the Indiction had been required in documents by a rescript of Justinian of 537[1], and the practice was adopted by the Popes at least as early as 550[2]. It was never used by them after the winter of 781. Hadrian also introduced a new and conspicuous feature into the structure of his documents drawn up in the more solemn form. He separated the work of the writer from that of the superior officer who 'dated' it, that is, who certified the Pope's subscription. The first was the business of the ordinary notary; the second task belonged to one of the six officers of the Chancery, who was responsible for the authenticity and the completion of the document. This Data or Datum is derived from the practice of the Roman Empire[3], but its revival in the

---

[1] Novell. xlvii. (Authent. Coll. v. 2).

[2] Mommsen, Das Römisch-Germanische Herrscherjahr, in Neues Archiv, xvi. (1891), 53 ff.

[3] Bresslau (ed. 1), i. 850.

form of a separate addition to the document appears to be due to Frankish influence ; and this explanation[1] is strongly confirmed by the precise time at which the change was made. Whatever be the meaning of Datum in other Chanceries, it may be laid down as established that with the Popes it did not indicate the delivery of the document to the recipient or to a messenger who was to take it to the recipient : it marked the final stage, the completion, of the document[2]. The distinction between the Scriptum and the Datum continues until the pontificate of Calixtus II ; but the Scriptum, for reasons which will be explained hereafter, had for some time earlier been passing into desuetude.

The Third Period begins with the pontificate of Leo IX, in 1049. This is marked by a striking and pictorial device distinguishing Privileges from Letters. A Privilege, or Great Bull, must show a circle on the left hand giving, among other things, the Pope's name ; this is called the Rota : and on the right it must bear the Pope's Farewell contracted into a large decorative Monogram, accompanied by an ornament called the Comma. It is usual to make a Fourth Period beginning with the accession of Innocent III in 1198 and continuing until the termination of the Great Schism by the election of Martin V in 1417, but such a period is marked by no change of form, but only by the establishment of complete uniformity and precision in the Papal Chancery,

---

[1] Bresslau (ed. 1), i. 869.
[2] *Ibid.* pp. 847 ff.

and by the accident that with the accession of Innocent III the regular series of Papal Registers begins. If a break is needed it would be best placed at the accession of Innocent II in 1130, when the regulation of the simpler, less ornamental, and more business-like forms of documents becomes more closely defined[1]. The modern Periods, the age of Briefs from Martin V to Sixtus IV, and that of the Motu Proprio from Innocent VIII to the present day, lie beyond the range of this work.

I now come to examine the elements of which a Papal Bull is composed. I have already explained that the word Bull properly indicates the leaden seal which was attached to the document. The document itself was described as *epistola, litterae, pagina, scriptum, privilegium, auctoritas, praeceptum,* the last three terms being reserved for special uses. We may call them Rescripts, but this name is never found in the documents. *Decretum* and *litterae decretales* also are sometimes employed; and the word *constitutum* or *constitutio,* which strictly does not mean a letter at all, but a document recording the Acts of a Synod presided over by a Pope[2], came to be applied to the Popes' letters after the eighth century. The choice among these various names was partly a matter

---

[1] See below, pp. 112–118.

[2] Such a document began with an Invocation and the Date, the names of the Pope who presided and of the members of the synod present. Then followed the record of the Acts of the synod, often including the text of documents read before it. At the end came the Pope's *subscripsi* and the Signatures of those present. See, for instance, Monumenta Moguntina, pp. 136 ff.

of fashion, but by degrees a Letter or Decree
came to be sharply distinguished from a Privilege,
and it is now usual to employ these two terms,
Privilege and Letter, to indicate the two main
types into which Papal documents fall. For
technical purposes it may be best to observe this
practice, though the older names of Great and
Little Bulls are still admissible, at least in English.
It must however be remembered that a Privilege
could be conferred by a Little Bull, and that all
Privileges were not necessarily of the nature of
title-deeds. The two types are clearly distinguished
by their formulae both in the First and Second
Periods, but it is not until the Third under Leo IX
—and even then not regularly—that Privileges
are marked out by a conspicuous difference of
external appearance.·

In describing the structure of a Bull I shall
retain the Latin names for the different parts,
because it is convenient to have a nomenclature
which is intelligible in all countries ; but I add
the English equivalents for more familiar use.

A Bull, as I have mentioned, consists for-
mally of a Text placed between two Protocols.
The opening Protocol states the Intitulatio, the
Pope's name and title, his name (without his
number[1]) followed almost invariably by the words
episcopus, servus servorum Dei. This may have
before it an Invocatio ; but it is seldom that this
is expressed in words. If it appears at all, it takes
the shape of a Chrism (☧) or a plain Cross. After
the title comes the Inscriptio or Address, giving

---

[1] The number came in with the Brief in the fifteenth century.

the name of the person or persons to whom the document is sent, and the Salutatio or Greeting. This greeting gradually assumes the form which has persisted down to modern times, *salutem et apostolicam benedictionem*; but some varieties may still be found, as *perpetuam in Domino salutem*[1] or the like. It was only used in Letters. Privileges have no Greeting: their Protocol ends with the solemn words *In Perpetuum*. Occasionally, perhaps through imitation of the Frankish emperors, the Pope gives his Title alone without Address or Greeting, and introduces the name of the person on whose behalf the document is drawn up, later on in the Narratio[2]. There were occasions too when the Pope expressly refrained from giving his blessing because the person whom he addressed was unworthy of it[3].

The Text may include four elements:

First, the Arenga, Proem, or Preamble, enunciates the obligation of the Pope's duty or authority. A large collection of such aphorisms existed, out of which a choice could be made of the formula appropriate to a particular case. Familiar examples are those beginning *Pie postulatio voluntatis effectu debet prosequente compleri*, &c. ; *Quotiens illud a nobis petitur quod religioni et honestati*

---

[1] Clement II for Bamberg, 1047: Acta, ii. 68 n. 103 [Jaffé, Reg. 4149].

[2] Thus John XIX for Grado, 1024: Acta, ii. 66 n. 101 [Jaffé, Reg. 4070].

[3] Alexander III to Count Miroslav, 1181, where the greeting is erased and the text begins, 'Quod tibi benedictionis alloquium non inpendimus, non de duritia nostra sed de tuis credas potius meritis provenire, qui ea te penitus reddidisti indignum': Acta, ii. 377 n. 431 [Jaffé, Reg. 14408].

convenire dinoscitur...; Apostolice sedis auctoritate debitoque compellimur. The Arenga had a sonorous ring in it which made the document start impressively. As increased care was given to the observance of rhythm, the balance of the phrases was skilfully modified and adjusted; and even after the best days of the Chancery were past and the style of its productions had degenerated Boniface VIII could still open a Bull with tremendous force: *Unam sanctam ecclesiam catholicam et ipsam apostolicam urgente fide credere cogimur et tenere*[1].

I take the next two elements in the document together. The Arenga is followed by the Narratio or Statement of the Case and the Dispositio or Enacting Clause. The Pope seldom makes a Promulgatio or Notification ('Be it known to you,' 'I would have you to know') as the Frankish sovereign did[2]. He proceeds straight to the Statement, and then to the Enacting Clause, his order or judgement thereon. But these two elements in the document were very often combined, the Enacting Clause including within it, in a relative or dependent clause, an indication of the particulars necessary for the understanding of the facts. Thus Alexander II writes to the Abbot of St Benedict at Taranto: 'Moved by

---

[1] The secret of the effect here is the heavy tread of the dissyllables at the opening. See below, pp. 80 f.

[2] As an exception I note Leo IX's Bull to the abbot of St Pierre au Mont (dio. Châlons), 1049, 'Idcirco noverit omnium presentium et futurorum regum et episcoporum seu omnium apostolice sedis fidelium unanimitas.' Acta, i. 12 n. 15 [Jaffé, Reg. 4184]. This was written at Rheims.

thy devout prayers, in which thou hast besought us to take under our apostolic protection the monastery which a certain Leucius built on his own land, we receive the said monastery under the guardianship of apostolic defence and confirm to it all its possessions[1].' In such cases the Enacting Clause was generally linked on to the Arenga by a conjunction or an adverb, 'Therefore,' 'And so,' 'Verily' (*Ideo, Eapropter, Quocirca, Itaque, Nos igitur, Inde est, Sane*). The Statement, when it appears as a separate sentence, describes with greater or less detail the situation with which the Pope has to deal. It may be that the rights of a monastery have been impugned : the house desires that they should receive protection. Or irregularities may have been reported which call for the Pope's intervention. Whatever the matter in question, it is stated at length. If abuses had to be spoken of, rhetoric demanded that they should be pictured in vigorous phrases, but we must not always accept these phrases as more than literary embellishments.

When the Statement is ended, the Pope makes his decision. The Dispositio, or Enacting Clause, according to the nature of the case, may take the form of a grant or confirmation of rights, of the grant of licence or dispensation, or of an appointment of delegates to enquire into disputed claims or alleged abuses. These three classes are those of Privilegia, of Litterae de Gratia (or Tituli), and of Litterae de Justitia (or Mandamenta), as they came in course of time to be distinguished.

---

[1] 1071: Acta, ii. 114 n. 149 [Jaffé, Reg. 4686].

Fourthly, it was necessary that a grant of privileges should be safeguarded and the enforcement of an order or judgement secured. This was done in the Final Clauses comprehended under the name of Sanctio. These may be three in number, all of which are found in a Bull of Gregory the Great for St Mary's at Autun[1]. First, the Sanctio proper, the Prohibitive Clause, which forbids any one to obstruct or contravene the execution of the Pope's will. It first appears as a participial clause, grammatically dependent on what goes before, but commonly beginning with a capital letter as though it were a new sentence : *Statuentes*[2], 'Enjoining under pain of excommunication that no man shall presume to do injury' to the monastery taken under the Pope's protection 'or to alienate its goods or possessions.' Gradually the form develops into a separate sentence, known from its opening words as the Nulli ergo. It runs after this fashion : *Nulli ergo omnino hominum liceat prefatam ecclesiam temere perturbare*, or according to another form : *Decernimus ergo ut nulli omnino hominum*, &c. Both these forms make their appearance in the second half of the eleventh century. The details of phraseology vary, and they were intentionally modified in order to improve the rhythm, but the sense remains the same.

---

[1] November 602, Reg. xiii. 12.

[2] The development of the formula may be traced in Bulls of Paul I for Monte Soratte, 761–2, in Cod. Carol. xxiii. (Monum. Germ., Epistt. iii. 526 f., 1892) [Jaffé, Reg. 2349], and of Sylvester II for St Saviour's on Monte Amiata, 1002, printed from a facsimile copy on papyrus in Spec. ii. 56 n. 92 [Jaffé, Reg. 3925].

The second clause is called the Penal Clause, or the Curse, or from its opening words the Si Quis : 'If anyone presume to attempt such a thing let him know that he will incur the wrath of Almighty God and of his blessed apostles Peter and Paul,' *Si quis autem hoc attemptare presumpserit, indignationem omnipotentis Dei et beatorum Petri et Pauli apostolorum eius se noverit incursurum*[1]. This form is sometimes elaborated, but seldom with the minute specification of penalties which we find in judicial sentences. An older type includes not only the threat of penalties to those who disturb the grant but also the assertion that the grant shall remain nevertheless firm and established : this is derived from an ancient Roman usage which persisted in private charters. *Quicunque autem hanc nostre concessionis praeceptionem violare praesumpserit, perpetuo anathematis vinculo religetur, et haec nostra concessio stabilis et firma permaneat*[2].

The third clause, which is less frequent, is the Benedictio, which promises a blessing to those who carry out the provisions of the charter : ' May the keeper of this privilege and the restorer and helper of the monastery aforesaid deserve to be enriched by reward blessed for ever and ever[3].'

[1] Alexander III for Beaune (dio. Autun): Acta, i. 259 n. 283 [Jaffé, Reg. 12627].

[2] Benedict VIII for Salerno, 1021: Acta, ii. 65 n. 99, from a copy [Jaffé, Reg. 4032]. Compare the form in Anglo-Saxon charters, *e.g.*, Oethilred A.D. 692–3 (Facsimiles of Ancient Charters in the British Museum, i. n. 2, 1873); and Regesto di Farfa, i. 25 A.D. 718.

[3] Leo IX for St Stephen's in Chieti, 1053: Acta, ii. 79 f., n. 113 [Jaffé, Reg. 4298 *a*]. Gregory I, Reg. XIII. 12, has 'Cunctis

The Text sometimes ends with the Apprecatio or Amen. It does not take the form of Feliciter which we find in Frankish documents. It is a simple Amen, sometimes repeated thrice, seldom twice. In the Triple Amen a difference of writing comes to be observed between the three words, each being written in a different type of character. The initial A is by turn a rustic capital, an uncial, and a curial cursive.

When the Text is thus completed, it needs the addition of the Pope's Subscription. This begins the final Protocol. So long as papyrus was used for the production of documents, this took the form of the words *Bene valete* written in full. It might be written either between the Scriptum and the Datum, or after them, or alongside of the Datum. From the beginning of the eleventh century it ceased as a rule to be autograph, though some apparently autograph specimens occur[1]. When it was not autograph, it was followed by three points (. .,) or by an abbreviated subscription (*ƒƒ*) in the Pope's handwriting[2]. It was superseded under Leo IX by the Monogram[3].

The second element of the final Protocol is the Scriptum, the record by the writer that the document is his work. It names the month but not the day or year on which the document was written ; the day was reserved for the last stage,

autem eidem loco iusta servantibus sit pax Domini nostri Iesu Christi, quatenus et hic fructum bonae actionis recipiant et apud districtum Iudicem praemia aeternae pacis inveniant.'

[1] Gregory VI, Spec. 13 (2).
[2] Benedict VIII, Spec. 10 (2).
[3] See above, p. 39.

the Datum. It names also the Indiction and the notary who drew up the document. I shall speak of the notaries later on in connexion with the changes in the Papal Chancery.

The last place in the document is occupied by the Datum. This names the day of the month in the Roman style, with the regnal year of the Emperor after 800, the Pontifical year, and occasionally from John XIII (968–970) the year of grace. It states that the document was 'given by the hand of' one of the higher officers of the Chancery, to whom I shall return later.

I may add two or three notes on points of chronology. First, when in December 781 Hadrian I gave up the mention of the regnal year of the Emperor in the East, he inserted before the pontifical year which he substituted for it a formula of great antiquity[1] which had not a chronological but a religious purport: it ran 'In the reign of our Lord God and Saviour Jesus Christ,' *Regnante Domino Deo et Salvatore nostro Iesu Christo cum Deo Patre et Spiritu Sancto per infinita* (or *immortalia*) *saecula*[2]. A similar but briefer form was used by John VIII for a short time after the death of the Emperor Lewis II in 875 and again for a short time before the coronation of Charles III.

---

[1] It is found in a shorter form in the seventh century collection of Marculf, xviii. (Monum. Germ., Formulae, 1886, p. 86), and in Anglo-Saxon and Italian charters of the eighth (Facsimiles of Anglo-Saxon Manuscripts, i. 1, 1868, from Canterbury; Regesto di Farfa, ii. 122, &c.).

[2] Baluze, Miscell., ed. Mansi, iii. 3 [Jaffé, Reg. 2435]; Mittarelli, Annales Camaldulenses, i. (1755), app. iii. p. 12, from an eleventh-century transcript [Jaffé, Reg. 2437].

Then follows a period of irregularity, until at the coronation of Otto the Great in 962 the Imperial year was restored. But it did not persist long. Under Conrad II it only once appears in a Privilege, and that when the Emperor was in Italy; under Henry III it is found but twice. Leo IX finally abolished it, and after his time no Imperial year is recorded in the Datum with two exceptions: one, a document of the Antipope Clement III in 1086[1]; the other, two documents of Paschal II after his humiliation by Henry V[2].

Secondly, the Indiction, which marks the position of the year in a cycle of fifteen years[3], has been reckoned at different times from the 1st of September, the 24th of September, and from Christmas. The Popes until the death of Victor III in 1087 admitted only the first of these : for all this period therefore the Indictional year begins four months in advance of what we should call the calendar year, only with the Popes this calendar year began not on the 1st of January[4] but a week earlier, on

---

[1] Mittarelli, iii. 39 f. [Jaffé, Reg. 5322].

[2] 'Romae in insula Lycaonia,' 15 April 1111, two days after the Imperial coronation: Monum. Bamberg. ed. Jaffé, 1869, pp. 277 ff., and Migne, clxiii. 286 f. [Jaffé, Reg. 6291, 6292]; Bresslau (ed. 1), i. 837 f.

[3] The first Indiction is generally supposed to begin in A.D. 312 (*i.e.* 1 September 311); but Otto Seeck has a good argument in favour of A.D. 297, Die Entstehung des Indictionencyclus, in the Deutsche Zeitschrift für Geschichtswissenschaft, XII. (1896), 279–296. The question is unimportant from a chronological point of view, for the number of the Indiction was never stated, but only the number of a given year within an unnamed cycle.

This date was expressly rejected on account of the pagan usages with which it was associated. See St Boniface's letter to Pope Zachary, Monum. Mogunt. p. 115, and the Pope's answer (April 743), pp. 120 f.

Christmas Day. But this mode of beginning the year cannot in fact be said to have prevailed except when the computation of years of the Christian era, *a nativitate Domini*, was adopted; and this was a reckoning which was introduced from England into the Frankish realm in the eighth century and passed to Rome, under Imperial influence, in the tenth[1]. It is first found in the pontificate of John XIII in 968, but it was only intermittently used before the time of Leo IX. In Papal documents preserved in originals errors in dating are not often found, but in transcripts we must be prepared for a confusion between the abbreviated forms, for instance, of January and June, or between the numerals *u* and *ii*[2].

The last stage in the production of the document was the attachment of the leaden seal or *bulla* by means of tags of parchment or more commonly of hempen or silk strings[3].

The description which I have given of the contents of a Papal document applies in strictness only to the more solemn form of the Privilege and of that down to the middle of the eleventh century; the number of simple Letters preserved in originals during this period is too small and the type is too little developed to enable us to lay down precise rules about their external structure.

[1] The Popes then seldom inserted the *annus Domini* except in documents addressed to churches in Germany.

[2] See Bresslau (ed. 1), i. 841, with whom I agree that apparent mistakes in date must not be hastily corrected: they are generally susceptible of explanation.

[3] The story in the Nouveau Traité de Diplomatique, iv. 298, v. 163 f., that Hadrian I was the first to order that Bulls should be sealed with lead, is traceable to Polydore Vergil, De Rerum Inventoribus, VIII. (pp. 654 f., ed. 1561). The authors of the Nouveau Traité have themselves abundantly refuted it.

III.

A remarkable document which in its existing form has been incorporated into several later compilations but which may be confidently assigned to the time of Otto III, describes the organization of the Roman notaries[1]. It enumerates seven Iudices Ordinarii or Palatini, as a clerical staff. They had their functions in the appointment of the Emperor and in the election, together with the Roman clergy, of the Pope. These seven Iudices were the Primicerius and Secundicerius Notariorum, the Arcarius, the Saccellarius, the Protus, the Primus Defensor, and the Amminiculator, the last name being a corruption of Nomenculator. All but one of these have already been described[2]. The exception is the Protus or Protoscriniarius, sometimes called the Primiscriniarius. We find no mention of him before 861[3]. It is clear that he was not a member of the College of Notaries and Scriniarii,—still less, as Galletti[4] and Hinschius[5] supposed, was he its

[1] See Appendix IV.

[2] Above, pp. 13–19.

[3] Galletti, Il Primicero, p. 134, says 827; but he relies on a Bull ascribed to Gregory IV, 20 June a. 1 (Jaffé, 2572), which was exposed by Muratori, Antiq. Italicae, iii. 40 ff., 1740.

[4] Il Primicero, p. 133.

[5] Kirchenrecht, i. 382.

chief. He might be and in more than one instance
is known to have been a layman. He belonged in
fact to a quite different department from that of
the Papal Notaries. He was the head of the
Tabelliones or public scriveners, whose duties were
regulated by the civil law[1], and who were placed
by it under the Magister Census.

In origin these Tabelliones had nothing to do
with the Church. But with the extension of the
Pope's local activity they became attached to his
staff and they are found signing their names as
Notarii et Tabelliones Urbis Romae. They formed
in fact a town guild, which gradually passed into
the service of the great government office established in the Pope's household. But they were not,
except in quite unusual circumstances, employed
for writing the Pope's documents: their business
was confined to drawing up deeds for private persons. In the tenth century they seemed to wish to
abandon the title of Tabelliones. They now called
themselves Scriniarii sanctae Romanae Ecclesiae[2].
But this description was known to be incorrect:
a gloss to the Decretals calls it *vulgare Romanorum*[3]. It involved a confusion with the Notarii
et Scriniarii Regionarii who ordinarily were alone
competent to write documents for the Pope. Still
the use of the word prevailed, and the Magister
Census was called the Protoscriniarius[4]. But though
he acquired this title, he was in no sense the head

[1] Novell. XLIV.

[2] Regesto Sublacense, pp. 162, 193.

[3] Gloss to cap. Ad audientiam, lib. II. Decretal. de Praescript.,
ap. F. Oesterley, Das deutsche Notariat, i. 88 f., 1842.

[4] Regesto Sublacense, pp. 166 f.

of the Scriniarii et Notarii Regionarii, the proper
officers of the Papal Scrinium; and hence it
was possible for him to be a layman. In course
of time, however, the office became a clerical one,
and its holder ranked as one of the Iudices Palatini.

In reviewing the history of the organization
of the Papal Court, we notice that while originally
two or three of the principal officers were not,
or were not of necessity, notaries, the whole
body was known as the College of Notaries,
and the office as the Scrinium. The lowest in
rank was the Protoscriniarius, who had risen
above his older function as the head of the civic
scriveners and had become attached to the
Scrinium, but was still sharply distinguished
from the superior officers in that he had charge
only of the writing of documents: he was excluded
from the more responsible duty of dating, that
is of authenticating and completing documents
for publication or dispatch. These two stages
in the production of solemn Bulls were established
during the pontificate of Hadrian I[1]. In the
final Protocol there is now a settled usage of
separating the statement as to who wrote the
document and who dated it, and this distinction
between Scriptum and Data continued until the
twelfth century, when the Scriptum died out
under Calixtus II. The distinction between these
elements comes to possess a special palaeographical
interest; it also enables us to follow out the
part which the different Iudices Palatini took
in the preparation of documents.

[1] See above, pp. 20, 38 f.

The person who wrote the document is, as a rule, described as Notarius regionarius et Scriniarius sanctae Romanae Ecclesiae[1]. When this is not the case, the exception is due to peculiar circumstances. An interesting example is furnished during the pontificate of Leo VIII, who was set up by Otto the Great in 963 on the deposition of John XII. Leo was soon driven out; then John died in May 964, and the Roman party proceeded to elect Benedict V as his successor. The Emperor thereupon went with his army against Rome, with Pope Leo in his train, and took the city after a siege. Leo was restored on 23 June; and almost immediately he issued a document confirming a monastery in the north of Italy in its possessions[2]. But although he had recovered possession of the Lateran Palace, he had as yet no secretarial staff. Quite possibly the Notaries attached themselves to his rival. So he was obliged to employ one of the civic scriveners, a Tabellio, to draw up the document. In like manner, in 980 Benedict VII had to flee from Rome to Ravenna, and necessarily employed a local Tabellio[3]. Such exceptions have an historical interest; but they do not affect the rule that documents must be written by the Notaries. Generally, even in the greatest difficulties, the Popes tried to have their documents drawn up

---

[1] Thus Nicholas I, 863, Spec. 3. But *regionarius* may be omitted, as in Benedict III, 855, Spec. 2.

[2] Printed from a transcript in Acta, ii. 43, n. 82. The date is given 'tertio decimo mensis Iunii,' ten days before Leo's restoration. Possibly *Iunii* stands for *Iulii*.

[3] Ughelli, Italia sacra, ii. 599, ed. 1717; Bresslau, i. 226.

by their regular accustomed clerks. The writing was done by simple Scriniarii et Notarii, very seldom by any of the higher officers of the College. In early times, indeed, under Gregory the Great, there is evidence of the Secundicerius so acting; but so soon as the Protoscriniarius came to take charge of the writing, no officer of superior rank is normally found to intromit himself in this work.

The function of the higher officers was to date the document, that is to say, to ratify it and guarantee that it had the Pope's authority. They were, to use a later term, the Dataries. The proper officer for this purpose was the Primicerius notariorum; but he was too important a man to be able to act personally in all cases. He was often absent on diplomatic missions or otherwise engaged. Therefore his place was frequently taken by the Secundicerius[1] or by one of the four officers next in rank; but hardly ever by the Protoscriniarius.

The innovation made by Hadrian I had the object of providing greater accuracy and security in the texts of documents by requiring that they should pass through two sets of hands. But the disadvantage still remained that the whole work of the Chancery was carried out by the College of Notaries, a body of men who, though technically the officers of the Pope, came in fact to represent the aims and policy of the Roman nobility, to which most of them belonged. The

---

[1] 'Secundicerii sanctae sedis Apostolicae,' Benedict III, 855, Spec. 2.

Pope needed a personal subordinate, a secretary. This was found in the Librarian. Now the Papal Library had for many ages not been separated from the Archives. Both were in the charge of the Primicerius, the Saccellarius, or some other of the Iudices Palatini. But under Hadrian I a special Librarian makes his appearance; and from the first quarter of the ninth century, under Paschal I, he comes to act in dating documents[1]. His employment in the Chancery was found convenient when the Pope, as so often was the case, had trouble with the powerful Romans, and documents came to be more and more frequently dated not by a notary but by the Librarian[2]. The Librarian was the Pope's nominee, a man who ranked high in his confidence and stood outside the Roman professional circle. He was almost always a bishop, and after a time was regularly chosen from among the suburbicarian bishops. Once for a short while, in 877–878, two bishops, who are styled Missi et Apocrisiarii, act in his place; they are followed by the Bishop of Porto from 878–879. But as a rule it was the Librarian himself who had charge of the Chancery.

Thus the old Iudices Palatini found themselves excluded from its business. After the

---

[1] Until lately it has been believed that an officer styled Bibliothecarius et cancellarius ecclesiae Romanae dated two documents of Leo III in 799. The documents are admittedly spurious, but they were conceived to be modelled upon a genuine original. I follow Dr Bresslau, i. 212, note 1, in rejecting their evidence altogether.

[2] Thus John XIII, 967, Spec. 8.

coronation of Otto the Great in 962 only seven documents are known to have been dated by the Primicerius or the Nomenculator; no other of the officers is found. After 983 they disappear altogether, and only the Protoscriniarius is mentioned in the following century. They had indeed still their appointed functions at the coronation of the Emperor and retained certain powers as magistrates; but the Pope's secretariate had passed entirely into other hands. The title of the Primicerius was preserved longest, but the last holder of it in 1299 was not styled Primicerius Notariorum but Primicerius Iudicum. The other six are found mentioned for the last time at dates ranging between 1185 and 1217[1].

The reign of the Librarian continues substantially unbroken, with one brief interval; but the organization over which he presided entered in the first half of the eleventh century into a state of confusion, almost of revolution. The Popes were striving to hold their own amid contending forces, and elements of disturbance entered the Chancery from opposite sides. These were the Roman tradition, pressure from the nobles of Tusculum, the influence of the Imperial system. For 36 years, from 1012 to 1048, the Papacy was in the hands of members of the Tusculan family whose relations to the Empire were more friendly than they were to the citizens of Rome. All these factors threatened to break up the working

[1] See L. Halphen's lists, Études sur l'Administration de Rome au Moyen Âge (1907), pp. 89–146.

of the Chancery.   The forms in which documents were validated become altered, and it is long before an established type is attained.   The Cardinals begin to take part in their drawing up, and the diction is a mixture of old and new. The large number of documents of this period preserved in the original enables us to trace the details of their workmanship in a way that it is not possible to do for earlier times, and these particulars have been explored with a minuteness which I cannot here follow.   It must suffice to say that recent investigations have thrown a new and welcome light upon one of the most intricate episodes in the history of the Papacy[1].

At first the notaries, who still style themselves Notarii Regionarii et Scriniarii sanctae Romanae Ecclesiae, write in the time-honoured Curial hand[2].   This was a corrupt development of the Ancient Cursive, having affinities with the Beneventan script; but it had acquired in the schools of the Roman notaries a special artificial character.   It persists in the Chancery down to the beginning of the twelfth century; but it is gradually beaten out of the field by the beautiful Minuscule which was imported from the Imperial system, and which acquired in the Papal Chancery a delicacy and refinement unmatched elsewhere. It is the fight between the Roman Curial and

[1] See particularly Paul Kehr, Scrinium und Palatium, in the 6th Ergänzungsband of the Mittheilungen (1901), pp. 70–112, in the light of whose results I have rewritten my account of this matter.

[2] Thus Sylvester II, 999, Spec. 9.

the Caroline Minuscule which furnishes the clue to the unravelling of the history of the Chancery in the eleventh century. The documents, I may add, continued to be written on papyrus beyond the middle of the century [1], though none is known to be preserved later than 1020–1022 in the pontificate of Benedict VIII; but parchment had come into use before his time [2].

I have said that on one occasion the Librarian was displaced by another officer. This was during the pontificate of John XVIII. Between December 1005 and May 1007 there are found seven documents of this Pope dated by the hand of Peter Abbas et Cancellarius Sacri Lateranensis Palatii, and three of them were not only dated but written by his hand [3]. That the same person should both write and date is a manifest anomaly, since the chief object of dating was to secure a double control. More striking is the substitution of the sacred Lateran Palace for the Holy Roman Church, which connects itself naturally with the introduction of the Frankish title of Chancellor [4]. It is the first authentic instance of the employment of the name by the Pope [5]; and it looks as though

[1] There is mention of a papyrus Bull of Victor II, in 1057: Marini, I Papiri diplom. pp. 86 ff., n. 50, and p. 241.

[2] See Bresslau's paper on Papyrus und Pergament in der päpstlichen Kanzlei, in the Mittheilungen, ix. (1888), 1–30.

[3] Spec. 10, *datum et scriptum per manum Petri abbatis et cancellarii sacri palatii* (here without *Lateranensis*), 1005.

[4] It is clear that Peter was not a deputy acting in the absence of the Librarian; for previously the Librarian had often been away, but his place was taken by a suburbicarian Bishop acting in his stead.

[5] See above, p. 56, note 1.

John XVIII not only appointed a new secretary with an Imperial title, but also established a staff of clerks of his own, his personal dependents, as distinguished from the official, almost here- ditary, staff of the Scrinium. But it would be unwise to draw any such large inferences; for the appointment may have been dictated by John Crescentius, the Pope's master: indeed, our knowledge of the years in question is so defective that we cannot say whether or not the Pope may not have been absent from Rome, and being thus deprived of his regular staff may have been obliged to make use of the services of some one in attendance on him. However this may be, John XVIII's practice was not continued.

A step of a different nature, but one which equally involved the removal of a suburbicarian Bishop from the Librarianship, was taken in 1023 when Peregrine, or Pilgrim, Archbishop of Cologne, was in Italy and Benedict VIII appointed him Librarian. It has even been supposed that the intention was to confer upon the occupant of the See of Cologne the permanent dignity of Chancellor, just as the Archbishop of Mainz held the analogous post of Royal Arch-Chaplain in Germany. But it is difficult to make this out. It looks rather as though the Pope merely desired to give Peregrine a conspicuous mark of honour. There is no evidence that the Archbishop ever performed the duties of Librarian in person. He appointed the Bishop of Porto to act for him, and the only documents of the time immediately following are dated by him in Peregrine's place, *vice Pelegrini archiepiscopi Coloniensis*[1]. Not long afterwards both Benedict VIII and the Emperor Henry II died, and the close ties which had for the moment bound together the Papacy and the Empire were broken. Benedict was succeeded by his brother, John XIX, who ignored the position of the Archbishop of Cologne. He did not indeed restore the old Scrinium, but he placed the Chancery once more under the management of suburbicarian Bishops; and only once, in December 1026, when Archbishop Peregrine was himself in Italy in the train of the Emperor Conrad II, do we find his position as Librarian recognized[2]. He lived for nearly ten years more, but there are no further traces of his title of Librarian. It was a quarter of a century later that the project of associating the Archbishop of Cologne, as such, with the Chancery was revived.

In the meanwhile, under the next Pope, Benedict IX, it was expressly ordained that one specified suburbicarian Bishop, the Bishop of Selva Candida, and all his successors should hold the office of Librarian[3]. This was done in November 1037, at a time when not only Conrad II but also Peregrine's successor Herman of Cologne were actually in Italy; so that the design of the ordinance cannot be misunderstood.

---

[1] A different form stating that the Archbishop appointed him is quoted by Dr Bresslau, i. 220, note 3; see too Spec. 10.

[2] Dat. per manus Benedicti Episcopi Portuensis vice Peregrini Coloniensis archiepiscopi bibliotecarii sanctae apostolicae sedis: Marini, p. 78, n. 46 [Jaffé, 4076].

[3] Marini, p. 83, n. 48 [Jaffé, n. 4110].

As, however, Benedict was a mere boy at the time[1], we must probably attribute to the permanent staff a measure directed against German influence at the very time when that influence was being exerted in a particularly vigorous fashion. The enactment was indeed shortlived: it was superseded five years afterwards, under the same Pope; but it was changed not in favour of the Imperial connexion, still less in that of the old Roman tradition. The suburbicarian Bishop was better than the old College of Notaries; but better still would be an officer appointed by the Pope of his own choice, a personal secretary[2]. Representing the Tusculan faction Benedict had always been unpopular at Rome, and more than once had been driven out of the city. It was all the more necessary that he should not rely upon the local officers. So he set up Peter the Deacon as Librarian and Chancellor, Bibliothecarius et Cancellarius sanctae Sedis Apostolicae; and Peter retained the position under his three successors. Moreover the appearance of this new Librarian and Chancellor is accompanied by that of two scribes bearing a new title. They subscribe the documents as Scriniarii et Notarii sacri Lateranensis Palatii[3]. The Pope was forming for him-

---

[1] At his election in 1033 Benedict is said by Rodulf Glaber (Hist. IV. v. 17) to have been 'puer ferme decennis.' Another account makes him twelve years old (*ibid.* v. v. 26).

[2] Dr Bresslau thinks that the Bishop of Selva Candida remained technically Bibliothecarius, but that his work was practically taken over by the Bibliothecarius et Cancellarius: i. 223 f. But Chancellor Peter does not date in anyone's stead.

[3] Or nostri palatii, Gregory VI, 1045, Spec. 13 (twice).

self a new clerical staff, attached to his person and unconnected with the old organisation of Rome. Still, however, they adhere to the Curial style of writing, so that they must have been recruited from Roman sources.

The intervention of the Emperor Henry III in 1046, the deposition of the rival Popes, and the establishment of the German Clement II, led to no immediate change in the Chancery. Peter, Librarian and Chancellor, remained at his post down to the pontificate of Leo IX[1], until his death in October 1050. But it is interesting to notice that an officer of the Imperial Chancery, whose handwriting is known from documents which he wrote for Henry when he was at Rome in the winter of 1046–7, was employed by the new Pope and drew up two of his documents of which the originals are preserved[2]. The fact was that Clement was travelling about in Italy with the Emperor and had no Roman notary available.

In such a manner non-Roman elements came to enter into the composition of the Pope's secretarial office. The change was not directly a political one, though it was influenced by political conditions. Quite possibly it was due to an imitation of the practice of the Emperors that the Popes sought to create a personal staff which should not be necessarily fixed at Rome. The Emperors had no one capital or residence, and their Chancery accompanied them from place

[1] Thus, 29 December 1046 and 24 September 1047, Spec. 14.
[2] The second example in Spec. 14.

to place. To the Popes on the contrary Rome had been their single and unchanging home. The head of his Chancery was a Bishop from the neighbouring district; its staff was formed of local officers attached to their district and church. They had to accompany the Pope when he quitted Rome for a time; but hitherto such absences had been the exception and had not lasted long. From the middle of the eleventh century on the contrary the Popes came to make protracted journeys away from the city; and they found the old local organisation ill-adapted to the new circumstances. Benedict IX began the change with his personal Chancellor and his personal staff of palace notaries. Clement II introduced notaries from outside Rome. The foreign notaries brought in their own handwriting, the Minuscule, because they were not conversant with the Curial style[1]. But when the Popes were at Rome they still to a large extent employed the old staff of Scriniarii. We gradually discover two distinct organisations going on at the same time.

1. The Scrinium, whose officers use the Curial hand and generally write the note of the Scriptum. In course of time they evolve a new title, compounded of the older and newer systems, and sign as Scriniarii regionarii et Notarii sacri Palatii. They remain permanently fixed at Rome.

2. The Sacrum Palatium, whose officers are attached not to the city of Rome but to the Pope's person, who attend him on his journeys away from Rome, and who, when he is in Rome, take

---

[1] See for instance two pieces of the year 1047, in Spec. 16.

part concurrently with the local Scriniarii in carrying on the business of the Chancery. They did not know the Curial handwriting and were not specially interested in maintaining the Roman tradition. They but gradually adopted the practice of writing the Scriptum, and even then only inserted it by way of exception. They style themselves not Scriniarii Regionarii but simply Notarii sacri Palatii and later on Scriptores. Standing as they did in a personal relation to the Pope, they could take upon themselves, as no Scriniarius ever ventured, to date a document as the representative of the Chancellor.

The pontificate of Leo IX—Bruno, Bishop of Toul—introduced important changes into the system and forms of the Chancery. The Pope was no longer a Roman official; he had to exert his influence over a wide sphere of Western Europe. He quitted Rome in May 1049, barely three months after his consecration[1], and from that time was always travelling. During a pontificate of more than five years he spent hardly more than six months altogether in the city. The Chancellor Peter he retained from his predecessor, and he took him about with him on his journeys. Peter not merely draughted and dated the documents but drew up the fair copy himself[2]. But so large was the number of privileges which the Pope granted that he had to appoint a writer

---

[1] During these months documents were written in the old style by a Scriniarius.

[2] Thus, 13 June 1049, Spec. 17 (1).

to help him [1]. This writer was a German named
Lietbuin and he naturally wrote a Minuscule
script [2]. When the Pope returned to Rome in
April and May, 1050, he avoided employing any
Roman writers [3]. After his next journey he
appointed Frederick Archdeacon of Liége (afterwards Cardinal and Pope, as Stephen IX) as
Bibliothecarius et Cancellarius [4], but for a while
he appears to have taken no personal share
in the work of the Chancery. About this time [5]
Leo conferred the dignity of Arch-Chancellor of
the Apostolic See upon Herman, Archbishop of
Cologne, who was *ex officio* the Imperial Arch-
Chancellor of Italy. The new title was plainly
borrowed from the usage of the Imperial Chan-

---

[1] In September 1049.

[2] Other writers were from time to time employed. One
was the famous Humbert, afterwards Bishop of Selva Candida.

[3] Thus, 29 May 1050, Spec. 19. On leaving Rome in the
summer he took with him a notary who was apparently an
Italian but not a Roman. He wrote a Minuscule modelled
upon that of the Chancellor Peter (19 July, Spec. 19). On
Peter's death at Langres in October this unnamed notary
acquired the right of dating documents in his own hand, but
of course in the name of the titular head of the Chancery. Peter
was followed by a member of a great Lotharingian family,
Udo Primicerius (afterwards, in 1154, Bishop) of Toul; but the
anonymous writer did his work for him and wrote the Datum
(Spec. 20) from October 1050 to January 1051, and later on
when Frederick was Chancellor. He disappears after 3 February
1052, and is followed by two writers in succession, neither of
whom was a Roman. But their position was less assured than
that of their predecessor, and for a time the Chancellor intervenes
personally to date the documents (9 March 1052, Spec. 21 (4),
cf. Acta ii. 76). Other scribes were also employed. See Kehr,
ubi supra, pp. 82 ff.

[4] Thus, 22 July 1051, Spec. 21.

[5] The Papal biographer says in June 1049.

cery; and it was not granted, as it had been in
1023, to a particular Archbishop of Cologne, but
was intended to be attached permanently to
the occupant of the See. There is, however,
no evidence that he ever acted in the Chancery.
He received the honour of the dignity and the
profits attached to it; but the dating was done
by Chancellor Frederick[1]. Yet it is to be noticed
that, while Leo IX seems to have done everything in his power to break off from the Roman
tradition, there is evidence, during the time that
he was again in Rome early in 1053, of the employment of Scriniarii; and these Scriniarii now
describe themselves by the remarkable style of
Scriniarii sacri Palatii.

I have dwelled at some length on the modifications of practice introduced by Leo IX, because
they show a resolute attempt to establish the
titles, the forms, the officials, and the handwriting of the Imperial Chancery in that of
the Pope. Over his immediate successors I shall
pass rapidly. With them it is local conditions
rather than policy that determine the employment of officials. Victor II (1055–1057) dismissed
Chancellor Frederick who was treated as an enemy
by the Emperor Henry III, and the Chancery
fell into disorder[2]; but during the three short

---

[1] In January 1054 Frederick departed for Constantinople,
and we do not know what arrangements were made during
his absence. Only two documents of that time are known to
be extant, and they are preserved in defective copies. See
Kehr, p. 85.

[2] Victor at first availed himself of the services of the Subdeacon Hildebrand, the future Gregory VII, and then on his

intervals at which he was at Rome he made use of the Scrinium with its old officers and forms [1]. The reorganization aimed at by Leo IX broke down partly in consequence of Victor's repeated changes of residence and partly through the removal from office of the Chancellor Frederick. When however Frederick became Pope as Stephen IX (1057–1058) and appointed Humbert Bishop of Selva Candida as his Chancellor and Librarian, the old Roman system again prevailed, though not exclusively [2]. His successor, the Tusculan Benedict X, was wholly Roman during the ten months that he was allowed to rule [3]. Nicholas II (1059–1061) also began with Roman Scriniarii [4],

visit to Germany employed the deacon Aribo, probably a Bavarian (9 February 1057, Spec. 25). The name of the Archbishop of Cologne is not regularly mentioned; the documents are usually dated by the writers themselves, one by Aribo; and the dates on the only two documents of this pontificate bearing Hildebrand's name are certainly not autograph (one, of 2 January 1056, is given in Spec. 24).

[1] The writer was *Gregorius notarius et scriniarius sanctae Romanae ecclesiae*. As soon as the Pope left the city the Roman writing ceased.

[2] The Pope lived partly at Rome and partly at Monte Cassino: he may have taken a Roman Scriniarius with him to his monastery, but he certainly employed another writer who was not a Roman as well. See documents of 2 November, 4 December, and 18 October 1057, in Spec. 27, 28. Under Stephen IX, it should be noticed, the dates of Cardinal Humbert are regularly autograph.

[3] He was finally excluded from the list of Popes, by a commission of which the late Cardinal Ferrata was president, in 1913. Two documents of his are preserved: one written by Octavian the Scriniarius; the other, written and dated by the same Lietbuin who had been employed as writer by Leo IX some ten years earlier (Spec. 28).

[4] Thus, 17 February 1059, Spec. 29.

but unlike his predecessors he took one of them away with him when he quitted the city for journeys in central Italy. When however, in November 1059, the Pope established himself in Florence, Florentine scribes were employed[1]. Humbert continued to be Librarian until his death on 5 May 1061; then for a few months his work was done by Bishops of two other suburbicarian Sees, Mainard, his successor at Selva Candida, and Bernard of Palestrina; but the office of Librarian seems not to have been filled up[2].

The pontificate of Alexander II which extended from October 1061 to 1073 is peculiarly anomalous. On his election he found himself confronted by an Antipope[3] and retired to his See of Lucca. His documents therefore present a double character: some of them are issued by the Pope, others by the Bishop of Lucca. I note this merely by the way, for we are only concerned with his Papal documents. But living at Luccà Alexander had to employ local scribes, sometimes from Florence[4], sometimes from Lucca: one document seems to be written by a notary of the Imperial Chancery. Still, in spite of irregularities, a type was growing up, with Majuscule letters in the first line and Minuscule in the rest; and the special characteristic feature was that the name of the Pope,

---

[1] See five examples in Spec. 30.

[2] Bernard possibly presumed upon his position, for at Benevento in June he was described as *cancellarius domini papae*: see Kehr, p. 93, note 4.

[3] Of this Pontiff, Cadalus or Honorius II, only a single *iudicatum* is known to exist: *ibid.*, note 5.

[4] Spec. 31.

between the Rota and the Monogram, was written
in square capitals. But when, early in 1063,
Alexander took possession of Rome he availed
himself once more of the Scrinium. There are
documents written by two Scriniarii, Rainer and
Guinizo, each of whom subscribes himself in the
lately devised composite form of Scriniarius et
Notarius sacri Palatii, and uses a Curial hand[1].
In his later stays in Rome also, in 1065, 1068, and
1069, the local notaries were again employed[2],
and one of them goes back to the older style
of Notarius Regionarius et Scriniarius sanctae
Romanae Ecclesiae, or, in a blundered form, of
Notarius et Regionarius ac Scriniarius sanctae
Sedis Apostolicae. On the other hand when he
was in Rome in 1070 and 1071 Alexander seems
not to have returned to the use of Roman writers;
he now, just as when he was away from Rome,
retained his notary from Lucca, whose handwriting can be clearly distinguished[3]. After 1063
a suburbicarian Bishop was no longer Librarian
and Chancellor: his place was taken by a simple
acolyte named Peter, who rose through the
successive orders until in 1070 he was made
Cardinal Priest of St Maria Nova[4]; he retained
office through the pontificate of Gregory VII.

[1] After he left Rome in 1064 his documents are no longer
written by Roman scribes: see Spec. 32.

[2] Illustrations of the handwriting may be found in Spec. 36
(1069).

[3] 3 March 1073, Spec. 39.   This notary was afterwards
the favourite scribe of Gregory VII.   His comma is characteristic: see Spec. 39.

[4] His data are usually autograph; when anyone takes
his place, he seems to be always a notary from Lucca.

From 1064 the dignity of the Archbishop of Cologne
as Arch-Chancellor is only intermittently recognized on the documents, and from May 1067 it
disappears. It ceases in fact concurrently with
the displacement of the Bishop of Selva Candida[1].
It may be said that Alexander II had no Chancery
system, and this was largely due to the fact that
he continued until the last to be Bishop of Lucca.

The pontificate of Gregory VII was uneventful
from the point of view of the Chancery: first
because Rome was his ordinary residence; and
secondly because his active policy called more
for the issue of Letters than of Privileges, of
Little than of Great Bulls. Of Privileges he
granted only about one-third the number of those
of his predecessor; and Letters were not protected
by the same elaboration of Chancery guarantee
as Privileges. Out of about 70 Privileges only
some 25 are known to be preserved in originals.
Most of them are written by the same notary
who had attended Alexander II from Lucca,
one Rainerius[2], who slowly learned the Curial
hand and never wrote it well. He put the Pope's
name in Majuscules, and often placed the Rota
in the middle of the sheet under the text. That
he was not a Scriniarius is shown by the facts
not only that he occasionally writes documents
away from Rome, but also that in the absence

---

[1] The name of the Archbishop of Cologne is found again
in two isolated documents of 1111 (just as the Imperial regnal
year was for the moment revived) when Paschal II was in the
hands of the Emperor, but never afterwards.

[2] 1078, Spec. 40.

of the Librarian he sometimes dates them[1].
This seems to mark a decided break from the
earlier tradition; yet there are also found traces
of the employment of the old Scrinium. It
has been supposed that Gregory maintained the
Curial handwriting as a witness that he was
Roman in policy and resolved to withstand the
importation of the Imperial Minuscule. But this
theory is unfounded. We have a number of
his documents written in Minuscule, and there
is no doubt that he himself wrote Minuscule[2].
It was in fact largely a matter of accident which
clerk he employed: the details of the Chancery
did not interest him[3].

Passing by the brief pontificate of Victor III[4]
we find under his two successors the alternation
of the old and new systems illustrated by a large
number of originals. Urban II was elected in
March 1088 at Terracina and did not enter Rome

[1] The head of the Chancery was still the Librarian, Cardinal
Peter; but other persons, Gregory the Deacon, Cono Cardinal
Priest, John Cardinal Deacon, often acted as his deputies.
They all most commonly wrote the data with their own hands.

[2] See his subscription, June 1057, Spec. 26; and Kehr's
references, p. 100, note 3.

[3] It may be mentioned that the only two known documents
of the Antipope Guibert of Ravenna (Clement III) are in Minuscule (Spec. 42). Probably they were written by any clerks
he could find at Cesena or Montebello. One written at Rome
is preserved in a transcript: see Kehr, p. 102.

[4] But one privilege granted by him is preserved, and that
not in the original: see Kehr, p. 103. The importance of this
Pope must not be judged by what he did during the four months
that he occupied the holy See. As Abbot Desiderius of Monte
Cassino his influence had been powerfully and continuously
exerted.

until the following October. While he was at
Rome we find a document written by Gerard
a Notarius Regionarius. In July 1089 the Pope
went southwards, and then two of his documents
were written and dated by the same hand, probably
that of the Prosignator and Chancellor John.
No one else being available, the Chancellor had
to be himself the engrosser. In the first half
of 1090 Urban was in Rome, and his documents
are written by a Scriniarius, Gregory, and in
the Curial hand[1]. But when he was away from
the city in 1092 and 1093, a new notary makes
his appearance; and he is the inventor of the
beautiful Minuscule which came to prevail for
the century following. Sometimes he dates the
documents, and gives his name, Lanfranc[2]. On
the Pope's return to Rome at the beginning
of 1094 the Scrinium reappears, and the writer
uniformly inserts the Scriptum[3]. We can trace
his work exactly when Urban was in Rome and
never when he was out of Rome. In the autumn
he went to the North of Italy and to France,
and was not again in Rome until Christmas
1096: all this time Lanfranc acted exclusively
as Scriptor for the Pope.

Under Paschal II we note the same characteristics: in Rome, the Scrinium; outside, the

---

[1] Thus 6 March 1090, Spec. 43.

[2] 26 January, 1092, Spec. 43; 1 February, 1092, Spec. 45.

[3] This writer, Peter, and the others who appear in Urban's
documents bear the title of Notarius regionarius et Scriniarius
sacri Palatii, or Scriniarius sanctae Romanae Ecclesiae, or simply
Scriniarius. Lanfranc is Notarius sacri Palatii; unlike the
Scriniarii he can date. See Kehr, pp. 105 f.

Palatium. But the handwriting of the one becomes modified by the other; the Curial hand borrows features from the Minuscule, and the Minuscule absorbs Curial elements[1]. The Palace staff, however, and the writing which it represented prevailed more and more. After Paschal II if any Roman notaries are employed they have to adopt the forms prescribed by the officials of the Palatium and omit the Scriptum. They retained indeed some features of the Curial hand, but these gradually disappeared. The suppression of the Scriptum is the mark of the victory of the Palatium over the Scrinium. It is accomplished under Calixtus II[2].

As for the head of the office Gregory VII's Chancellor, Peter, went over to the Antipope, and Urban II had to find a substitute. He chose a monk of Monte Cassino, John of Gaetà, Cardinal Deacon of St Mary in Cosmedin, and appointed him first Prosignator[3] and then in September

---

[1] In the Scrinium Peter was followed by John and Rainerius, Gervase and Bonushomo. For Peter's writing see Spec. 47; John's, 50; . Rainerius, 51, 53; Gervase (1115), 55. In the Palatium Grisogonus is the only notary named, because he is found to write the Scriptum; but five others have been discriminated.

[2] This fact has led some writers to make a subdivision of the Third Period in the history of the Chancery at his pontificate.

[3] The meaning of this name is not certain, but it is probable that it indicates the share taken by the official in the authentication of a Bull. This, it is considered, would be done by the completion of the Rota, in the inner part of which the Pope wrote his Device, and the officer added the writing on the circumference. See Bresslau, i. 268, note 1; Kehr, pp. 95, note 3, and 106, note 2. The practice, however, was not uniform; see below, p. 108.

1089 Chancellor: he held the office for thirty years, and always wrote the Datum with his own hand[1]. Finally he became Pope, as Gelasius II, in 1118. He set a memorable landmark in the history of the Chancery, not by altering its system but by renovating its style. This style must be the subject of a separate treatment.

---

[1] When a substitute acted for him the Scriptum and Datum are sometimes combined.

IV[1].

The fact that the composition of Papal letters
was governed by precise and elaborate rules
determining the rhythmical proportion and the
cadence of each period is a discovery of compara-
tively recent years. The system, known as the
Cursus Curiae Romanae, was perfectly understood
and was repeatedly expounded in the middle
ages; but because it was based not on metre
but on accent, and because its interpreters used
metrical terms for its exposition, the scholars of
the Renaissance, having found out the meaning
of quantity, rejected it with contempt and assidu-
ously avoided the use of any of the phrases which
it prescribed. Hence, except in some time-
honoured formulae or in liturgical cadences, which
were retained from their familiarity, we find
that the cultivated Latin of the modern age,
whether issuing from the Papal Chancery or
elsewhere, studiously arranges to end its clauses
or periods in a way which would not have been
permitted by the rules of the medieval chancery.
The system thus superseded passed not only
out of use but out of knowledge.

[1] The draught of this lecture was composed more than
fifteen years ago, but it has been several times rewritten and
in the end vitally modified by the results as to the ancient Cursus
obtained by Professor Zielinski of Petrograd and by Mr A. C. Clark,
now Professor of Latin at Oxford.

It was indeed observed by Wattenbach in 1855 [1] that an affected sort of prose was developed for epistolary purposes by Alberic of Monte Cassino as early as the eleventh century, and in 1868 Charles Thurot pointed out that the rhetorician Buoncompagno in the thirteenth mentioned the *artificiosa dictionum structura* which some called *cursus* [2]. Then in 1870 M. Paul Meyer indicated that this style must go back at least to the beginning of the twelfth century and hinted that its examination would be of great value for critical purposes [3]. But the suggestion was not seriously taken up until M. Noël Valois published his classical essay on the Rhythm of Papal Bulls in 1881 [4]. The new element in the enquiry is strictly limited. It is not Dictamen as a whole, but one particular feature in Dictamen. Dictamen or the Ars Dictandi is the name given to the instruction in letter-writing which was a subject of special study in the schools of

[1] Iter Austriacum 1853, in the Archiv für die Kunde Österreichischer Geschichts-Quellen, xiv. 34 f.

[2] 'Appositio, que dicitur esse artificiosa dictionum structura, ideo a quibusdam cursus vocatur, quia, cum artificialiter dictiones locantur, currere sonitu delectabili per aures videntur cum beneplacito auditorum': Histoire des Doctrines grammaticales au Moyen Âge, in Notices et Extraits des Manuscrits, xxii. ii. 480.

[3] 'On comprend maintenant de quel instrument précieux la critique sera pourvue lorsqu'on aura déterminé l'époque où le *cursus* se montre pour la première fois et les combinaisons employées par chaque auteur': Revue critique d'Histoire et de Littérature, v. i. 220.

[4] Bibliothèque de l'École des Chartes, xlii. 161–198, 257–272. When it first appeared as an academic thesis in 1880, a reviewer described the subject as 'assez curieux, bien que peu attrayant': Revue critique, xv. i. (1881), 324.

the middle ages. Treatises in which the doctrine is set forth are in like manner entitled Dictamen or Ars Dictandi[1], Summa Dictaminis[2], Forma Dictandi[3]. The definition of its province may be thus stated.

Grammar taught the correct use of words; Rhetoric, the appropriate combination of words in phrases and sentences: Dictamen dealt with a particular branch of Rhetoric, the rules of composition primarily as applied to the writing of letters, and of letters conceived in a more or less formal or ornamental style. The question of rhythm was not necessarily involved in it, but when the system of the Cursus became fully developed, it was considered as an integral part of Dictamen; so that a writer of the early years of the fourteenth century could speak of 'this literary Dictamen, which is neither altogether prose, nor altogether metrical, but participates in both[4].' It is the history of this rhythmical prose which we have now to examine; and I shall begin by quoting the rules for its composition as they were laid down in the Forma Dictandi of Albert of Morra and in the Dictamen of Trasimund. Albert was Chancellor to three Popes from 1178 to 1187, when he was himself elected

[1] By Trasimund: Valois, pp. 170, 171, note 2.
[2] By Pontius of Provence: Thurot, p. 38.
[3] By Albert of Morra, see below.
[4] 'In hoc vero dictamine litteratorio, quod nec est ex toto prosaycum nec ex toto metricum, sed utrumque participat': Bibliothèque nationale, MS Lat. 11,384 fo. 94, cited by Valois, p. 165, note 1. The work referred to is catalogued by Delisle as a Formulaire de lettres, à l'usage de l'ordre de Cîteaux: Bibliothèque de l'École des Chartes, xxiv. (1863), 232.

to the pontificate; and Trasimund, or Transmund, a Notary of the Holy Roman Church, acted as Albert's deputy[1], when he was perhaps sick or absent, from 9 December 1185 to 13 March 1186[2]. The two men were thus responsible for or connected with the preparation and issue of Papal documents at a time when the system of the Chancery, by common agreement, had attained or was just about to attain its highest perfection.

Albert's work begins with the words, *Cursus dictaminis Romane curie taliter observandus est*: the style to be explained is specifically that of the Roman court. Since Albert became Pope under the name of Gregory VIII the system which he described acquired the name of Stylus Gregorianus, a name which has led to not unnatural confusion. First something must be said of the prosody. The terminology belongs to a time when quantity had been for ordinary purposes superseded by accent. A man would still observe metrical rules if he wrote hexameters or other classical forms of verse; but he did this artificially: he pronounced the words by accent. And thus he came insensibly to use the traditional names of metrical feet to mean the equivalent number of syllables governed by accent, no matter what their quantity might be. Every dissyllable is a spondee; every trisyllable of which the penultima

---

[1] In one manuscript of his work he is described erroneously as vice-chancellor; others make him a monk (or even abbot) of Clairvaux: see Valois, pp. 168 f.

[2] Bresslau, i. 247.

is short (that is, unaccented) is a dactyl[1]: so that *mare* ranks as a spondee, *dominus* as a dactyl. This being understood, we pass to the rules laid down for the beginning and the body of the period or sentence, and for its ending. The rules concern only the Text of the document: the opening Address and Greeting, and the Date at the termination, fall outside the laws of Dictamen.

As to the closing phrases the rules are precise and fixed: for the beginning and middle we have only general directions.

If, says Albert[2], you begin with a spondee or with a trisyllable having the accent on the penultima, you may well follow with a dactyl, as *Deus omnium, Magister militum*[3]; but if you begin with a dactyl ('quod vix aut nunquam concedo,' adds Trasimund[4]), you must slacken the pace by several spondees, as *Dominus et magister noster Iesus Christus*. Two or more consecutive dactyls are forbidden; they are too rapid: thus *Negligens famulus aliquis*. But several spondees may follow one another. After a colon or a comma you may proceed either with a spondee or a dactyl.

---

[1] Thus Pontius of Provence in the thirteenth century: Thurot, p. 481.

[2] I summarize here from the passages printed by M. Valois, pp. 181 f.

[3] The former of these alternatives is forbidden by the Libellus de Arte Dictandi attributed to Peter of Blois, whose exposition is in other respects taken from Albert's: see the extract in M. C. V. Langlois' Formulaires de Lettres, iv. 12 (Notices et Extraits des Manuscrits, xxxiv. ii. 26, 1893). The same prohibition occurs in a thirteenth-century treatise (apparently based on Trasimund) in the Laurentian Library at Florence, from which M. Langlois gives a quotation, *ibid.* v. 6 (Notices et Extraits, xxxv. ii. 410, 1896).

[4] Valois, p. 182, note 4. But conjunctions like *Ideo, Igitur* were permitted: see Pontius, in Thurot, p. 481.

It is clear that it was held that the dignity of an opening phrase was best secured by the choice of a weighty dissyllable: *Sane, Dudum, Nobis,* and the like are frequently found in this position. Secondly, there was a feeling in favour of alternate accents, rather than of accents going by threes: a dactyl must be guarded by spondees, but spondees may be continuous. Albert omits to explain that unaccented, possibly slurred syllables may be introduced. Later writers called them half-spondees; often they may be reckoned as elements of dactyls[1]. But the matter is not important, for it is evident that no very strict rules were laid down in detail as to how a sentence should go on. How it should end, on the contrary, was a matter of unyielding law.

Albert lays down the rule as follows:

It is to be noted that a foot as it were a dactyl must always precede the final elements (*dictiones*). And the final element of a period should be a word of four syllables with the penultima long: as *Ad eterna mereamur gaúdia pèrveníre.* Or there may be at the end of the clause two words of two syllables, of whatever length they be: as *Inhumanitatis est nimiẹ in hominem ágere nìmis dúre.* Sometimes too a monosyllable and a trisyllable, preceded by a dactyl, end the period, so that the second syllable of the trisyllable has the accent: as *Donec per se suffíciant àd volátum*[2].

This describes the first of the admissible endings. It is a dactyl, followed by a word or combination of words of four syllables, in the language

---

[1] Monosyllabic words were regularly treated as enclitic or proclitic.

[2] Valois, pp. 188 f.

of the time two spondees. It is the termination
which came to be known as the Cursus Velox.
Albert proceeds:

> Sometimes again two trisyllables end the period: as
> *Petitiones honestas, ius, et ratio audíri compéllunt.* Sometimes
> it is a word of four syllables followed by a trisyllable: as
> *Quicquid adversus eum proposui, astruere confidénter audébo*[1].

This is the Cursus Planus. But Albert has confused the matter by talking of the length of the
words (*dictiones*) preceding the final trisyllable.
The point is that a concluding paroxytone word
of three syllables must be preceded by a word
of three or any number more syllables, of which
the penultima is long. To these two Trasimund
adds a third, which completes the series of
admissible endings. Albert had made no provision
for a dactylic termination; if such an ending is
required, Trasimund says that it must consist
of a word of four syllables with the accent on
the antepenultima (or a monosyllable and a
dactyl), preceded by a word accented on the
penultima: as *Ille certe videtur operári iustítiam,*
or *tunc facta dirigéntur in éxitus*[2]. This became
distinguished as the Cursus Tardus, also called
Durus or Ecclesiasticus.

These are the three forms with which a sentence
or principal clause invariably ends. They will
be most conveniently arranged, as they were
in fact in the thirteenth century[3], still retaining

---

[1] Valois, p. 189.

[2] *Ibid.* p. 193.

[3] See an extract in Thurot, p. 482, from a work which,
according to M. Valois, p. 173, note 2, is by Master Lawrence

the medieval names for the measures, in the following order:

1. Cursus Planus : dactyl + spondee   – ◡ | – – –
2. Cursus Tardus : dactyl + dactyl   – ◡ | – ◡ ◡
3. Cursus Velox : dactyl + 2 spondees   – ◡ ◡ | – – – –.

I reserve the explanation and analysis of the three types until a later stage, and only here lay emphasis on the caesura, which is duly noted, though not emphasized, by our earliest authorities. There must be a caesura before the last three syllables in the Cursus Planus, and before the last four syllables in the other two types.

Our authorities, I have said, worked in the second half of the twelfth century. From whom did they have their model[1]? So soon almost as the question was raised, Monsignor Duchesne supplied the answer[2] by a reference to one of the continuations of the Liber Pontificalis. In that work the appointment as Chancellor by Urban II of John of Gaetà, who afterwards became Pope

of the city of Rome, who was apparently connected with Aquileia (cf. L. Rockinger, Briefsteller und Formelbücher, i. 951 f., 1863).

[1] It was unlucky that M. Valois should have impaired the value of his admirable work, which must always be consulted for the period from the twelfth century onwards, by excursions into the early history of rhythmical composition. But in 1881 the distinction between the metrical and accentual systems had not formed the subject of detailed study, and M. Valois could not be aware that his remarks on the ancient rhythmical writers were not really relevant. He has, however, the merit of having observed correctly the ages during which some form of Cursus prevailed and the intermediate period during which it was neglected or even forgotten.

[2] Note sur l'Origine du 'Cursus,' in the Bibliothèque de l'École des Chartes, l. (1889), 162.

Gelasius II (1118–1119), is recorded by his contemporary biographer Pandulph in the following terms:

> Then the Pope, a well-lettered man and of ready speech, perceiving brother John to be both wise and prudent, ordained, promoted, and from careful deliberation appointed him his chancellor, so that through his eloquence which the Lord had granted him, John might under the guidance of the Holy Spirit by the grace of God reform the style of ancient grace and elegance in the apostolic see, which was now almost all lost, and might restore the Leonine rhythm with its lucid rapidity[1].

Here John of Gaetà is expressly stated to have been the author of the revival of the ancient Cursus, which is described, for what reason is not clear, as Leonine. Now it can hardly be a mere coincidence that at the same date the formulary which had been long in use in the Papal Chancery, the Liber Diurnus, suddenly disappears from view. It was used in 1087; it is not found afterwards. It looks as though, because its rhythm and periods were not those of the Cursus, John of Gaetà, as Prosignator and then as Chancellor, suppressed it.

---

[1] 'Ut per eloquentiam suam a Domino traditam antiqui leporis et elegantiae stilum in sede apostolica, iam pene omnem deperditum....reformaret, ac Leoninum cursum lucida velocitate reduceret': Lib. Pontif. CLXII. vol. ii. 311. In a continuation of the Liber Pontificalis preserved in the Harleian MS 633 (of the second half of the twelfth century) it is said of Gelasius II: 'Hic fuit in scripturis divinis vir eruditus, rectus, et multe simplicitatis, et ordinis atque consuetudinis sancte Romane ecclesie studiosissimus indagator, miserorum quoque adiutor piissimus.' See W. Levison, in Neues Archiv, xxv. (1910), 411. Professor Levison is inclined to connect the compilation from which the existing manuscript is copied with Archbishop Ralph of Canterbury (p. 421).

John was a disciple of Alberic of Monte Cassino in the Ars Dictandi. Alberic was a man of learning, who took an active part in the controversy aroused by the opinions of Berengar of Tours. He was a Cardinal Deacon, but there is no evidence that he was ever employed in the Papal Chancery. He might well have acted there, for he was an authority on Dictamen. He wrote two treatises on the subject, dealing with grammatical points and with rules for prose composition. These works may be dated about 1075 or a little earlier[1]. They begin with a classification of *dictamina* as *metrica, rithmica,* and *prosaica,* but the author expressly limits himself to this last variety[2], so that one cannot tell whether the other subjects formed part of his system of instruction. It is, however, certain that he employed the Cursus, though not uniformly, in his own compositions[3]; and this fact raises a presumption that it was from him that John of Gaetà learned the art which he introduced into the Roman Chancery. In any case, it need not be doubted that the Cursus came from Monte Cassino. John of Gaetà may have been there when Frederick of Lorraine, afterwards Stephen IX, was Abbot; he was professed there under Desiderius[4], who was Abbot

---

[1] See A. Bütow, Die Entwicklung der mittelalterlichen Briefsteller bis zur Mitte des 12. Jahrhunderts, a Greifswald dissertation of 1908, pp. 15–20.

[2] Rationes dictandi II. in Rockinger, i. 9.

[3] See the Rationes Dictandi and De Dictamine, *ibid.*, i. 9 ff., 29 ff.

[4] His biographer says, under the next abbot Oderisius (Lib.

until he became Pope as Victor III in 1087. It was a time of literary activity in the monastery. Desiderius caused the Registers of fifth-century Popes, now lost, to be copied out[1]; and the existing transcript of the Register of John VIII was made there very probably under the supervision of John of Gaetà himself. A contemporary monk, Leo, wrote letters for Urban II, and had to do with the composition of his Register[2]; and John of Gaetà had been engaged in literary production before he was called as Prosignator and then Chancellor to Rome. There are therefore many reasons for believing that John brought with him the Cursus into the Papal Chancery from a training which he had learned at Monte Cassino.

John of Gaetà's reform did not at once attain complete prevalence, and it was not until after the middle of the twelfth century that the rules of the Cursus were uniformly observed. In particular, men were slow to alter old-established formulae. Thus the clause *Nulli ergo omnino*

Pontif. clxii. vol. ii. 311); but the error is exposed by the editor, p. 318, notes 2 and 10. See Peter the Deacon, de Viris illustribus Casinensibus, xlv. (Migne, clxxiii. 1046).

[1] Chron. Monast. Casin., iii. 63, in Monum. Germ. hist., Scriptores, vii. 746.

[2] 'Scripsit ex nomine Urbani papae epistolas, fecit et registrum eius': Pet. Diac., de Viris illustr., xxxi. p. 1039. He may be the Leo, Cardinal Deacon, who dated documents for Paschal II: Jaffé, i. 702. But he is to be distinguished from Leo Marsicanus, afterwards Cardinal Bishop of Ostia, who wrote the continuation of Peter's Chronicle of Monte Cassino: see E. Caspar, Studien zum Register Johanus VIII, in Neues Archiv, xxxvi. (1911), 95, note 3.

hominum liceat hanc nostre constitutionis paginam infringere, or *Nulli ergo hominum fas sit hanc nostre constitutionis paginam ausu temerario refringere,* persisted until the middle of the twelfth century. But then by a slight modification the ending was set right; and we find *temerario ausu infringere* or *ausu temeritatis infringere,* or again *temere perturbare,* or by a somewhat larger change *hanc paginam nostre confirmationis infringere*[1]. Similar changes may be noted in other formulae; but these constituted the more rigid parts of the document and did not yield to the new rules as easily as the phrases which were elaborated afresh by the Dictator.

In 1892 M. Louis Havet endeavoured to explore the origin of the Cursus by means of a minute analysis of the clause-endings in the writings of Symmachus, a rhetorician of the last part of the fourth century[2]. He established beyond dispute that the principle here was that not of accent but of metrical quantity; but he was led on a false track by supposing that the rhetorical close must consist of entire words or groups of words. The truth is that it is composed of two metrical phrases and that these metrical phrases are formed out of feet which do not at all necessarily correspond to the division of separate words. M. Havet said in effect, You take a word of almost any number of syllables

---

[1] I take these examples from M. Valois, p. 260.

[2] La Prose métrique de Symmaque et les Origines métriques du Cursus.

or any form you please for the end of a clause,
and according to the form it bears it must be
preceded by a word of two or three syllables of
a prescribed measure[1]. The final word might
assume any one of twenty forms ranging from
one foot to three and a half, and the number
of its syllables determined the metrical form of
the word preceding, which might be a trochee,
an iambus, a pyrrhic, or a spondee, a tribrach,
an anapaest, a dactyl, or a cretic; each final
form being assorted with a choice of antecedent
forms. To state M. Havet's theory in this way
is to condemn it. It is infinitely too complicated for practical use. He deserves our
gratitude for his painstaking tabulation and
classification of the facts, but he did not
succeed in deducing from them a working
system.

A great step forward was taken by Dr Wilhelm
Meyer, of Spires, Professor at Göttingen, in the
year following the publication of M. Havet's
essay[2]. While doing full justice to the merits
of the work of the French scholar, he pointed
out its fundamental error. M. Havet's theory
depended upon entire words (or groups of words)
and made the form of the final word (or group)
determine the form of the word before it. But,
as Dr Meyer showed, it is not a question of the
combination of single words; it is the combination
of syllables which make up the close of a rhetorical

---

[1] See M. Havet's exposition, pp. 31–66, and the table on
pp. 111 f.

[2] Göttingische Gelehrte Anzeigen, 1893, pp. 1–27.

period, the Clausula Rhetorica[1]. We must not count the separate words, but consider the syllables or feet which compose the Clausula. The key to this he found in the Cretic, $(- \smile -)$ which from Cicero's time was regarded as constituting one of the two most appropriate schemes for ending a phrase; the other being the Ditrochaeus $(- \smile - \smile)$. We must give up all the medieval terminology of Dactyls and Spondees. The accentual Dactyl originates in a metrical Cretic, and the accentual Spondee comes from a metrical Trochee. The Clausula Rhetorica consists of a Cretic base followed by a Trochee, a Cretic, or a double Trochee[2].

It would not, however, be correct to say that these three terminations were the only ones allowed in early times. It was lawful to substitute for the Cretic three long syllables, a Molossus, for special emphasis; the first or the last syllable might be resolved into two short syllables, forming a Paeon; or again a Trochaic cadence might be prolonged by an additional syllable, making the close consist of a

---

[1] This is laid down by Quintilian: 'Nec solum refert quis [pes] claudat, etiam quis antecedat. Retrorsum autem neque plus tribus, iique si non ternas syllabas habebunt, repetendi erunt..., neque minus duobus; alioqui pes erit, non numerus': Inst. IX. iv. 95.

[2] Dr Meyer somewhat impaired the clearness of his exposition by avoiding the word Trochee, which he called a half-Cretic, and by treating the Ditrochaeus as an anomalous feature (a form of his 'free Cretic'). He also invented some needless irregularities, for instance, through carrying the Clausula too far back and so producing what he termed the 'inverted Cretic.' But the main principles which he laid down are quite established.

Cretic, a Trochee, and another Cretic. These variations indicate the flexibility of the system developed by the earlier rhetoricians. They gave free play to expression governed by the rules of an harmonious close. Thanks to the elaborate analysis of the terminations in Cicero's speeches made by Professor Zielinski[1], we are enabled to arrive at some precise results as to the proportion which the three main forms constitute to the total number of endings. If we admit the Molossus, they are found to be 60 per cent.; and if we allow a few other licences in the base, they come to nearly 87 per cent.

The Caesura in the ancient system was not invariable. Dr Zielinski has arranged a convenient system of notation to indicate the possible modes of dividing up the phrase. He calls the Cursus Planus, Tardus, and Velox, 1, 2, 3 (Professor Clark's happily chosen examples[2] are easy to remember,

    1. Víncla perfrégit;
    2. Víncla perfrégerat;
    3. Vínculum frègerámus).

Then he denotes the possible divisions by letters of the Greek alphabet. If the whole phrase is one word, it is *a*: *iudicabatur* is 1 *a*. If there is a Caesura before the second syllable,

---

[1] Das Clauselgesetz in Cicero's Reden, 1904. A summary of the author's results is given in a notice of the book by Mr Clark in the Classical Review, xviii. (1905), 164–172. Mr Clark's collection of texts and examples printed in his Fontes Prosae Numerosae (1909), and his paper on The Cursus in Mediaeval and Vulgar Latin (1910), are also invaluable.

[2] The Cursus, p. 10.

it is β, and so forth. In Mr Clark's examples *Vincla perfregit* is 1 γ; *Vincla perfregerat* is 2 γ; *Vinculum fregeramus* is 3 δ. Now in the ancient practice a great deal of freedom was allowed as to where the Caesura should fall. We find *Beatitúdine frúitur* (2 δ), *términos quaérit* (1 δ), and the like. But the three forms of Caesura which appear in the medieval Cursus show from very early times a marked preponderance. What is peculiar to the medieval system is the law that no other Caesura could be admitted.

It was supposed by M. Louis Havet that the medieval accentual Cursus arose from a misunderstanding of the ancient metrical system. The ancient system was observed down to the seventh century; it then fell into complete desuetude. It was forgotten, and was suddenly revived in a blundered form towards the end of the eleventh century. If the facts were true, the critical inferences to be drawn from them would be very valuable. For we should be in a position to decide the genuineness of many disputed texts assigned to a date between about 650 and about 1080: if they contained the metrical Cursus they were before the earlier date; if the accentual, they were after the later date. This critical canon for some years held the field[1]. But unluckily neither the facts nor consequently the inference drawn from them can be maintained.

[1] See Julien Havet, Œuvres, i. 312–317, 1896. It is right to mention that the paper there reprinted was left unfinished at the author's premature death in 1893.

So far from the accentual Cursus being an invention of the eleventh century, it can be traced back to ancient times as an element in the Sermo Vulgaris. It has been noticed in Vitruvius, Frontinus, and Petronius; and Mr Clark has made the very interesting discovery that it is a characteristic of the colloquial style of Cicero's letters to Atticus, in contrast with all his other writings[1]. The vulgar accent made inroads on the system of the metrical terminations. 'The result,' says Mr Clark, 'of the enfeeblement of quantity and the stress of the accent was to produce what some writers have called a *cursus mixtus*, a very convenient term which means that some of the clausulae are metrical, while others follow the accent without regard to the quantity. All that is necessary is to have the accents in the right place. The result is that the metrical prose of St Cyprian, Symmachus, and Sidonius gives way to accentual or rhythmical prose[2].' When the sense of quantity yielded before the pressure of accent, it was inevitable that the metrical forms which were inconsistent with accent should disappear and only those which admitted of an accentual treatment survive[3].

---

[1] The Cursus, pp. 26 f.

[2] p. 10.

[3] It would be out of place here, even did I profess the knowledge, to do more than advert to the fact that in Greece a similar system, based on prosody, is found as early as the Attic orators. It was by degrees modified in accordance with a change of pronunciation, and the result was not unlike that which came about in Latin. See Eduard Norden, Die antike Kunstprosa, 1898.

The Cursus of the Roman Chancery was therefore no new invention, still less a revival based on a misunderstanding of the ancient system. Its author, be he Alberic of Monte Cassino or some Italian before him, no doubt started from the study of the classical or sub-classical writers on rhetoric; but he adapted their rules to the facts of the pronunciation of his own day. He thus reflected an historical development: accent, not quantity, was the one element that could be considered. Beyond introducing the system as a rigid code for the Chancery, the only vital change made by John of Gaetà and his successors was not an innovation but a limitation. By forbidding any other Caesura than that now laid down for each of the three endings, they made less demands on the memory of the Dictator, but at the same time they deprived the Cursus of the variety and flexibility which it had possessed in early times. It was soon found that the strict rules excluded some sonorous phrases which on other grounds appeared well suited for the close of a period; these were after a time admitted exceptionally, but not in the purest period of the Chancery. Some of these licences are in fact the accentual representatives of ancient forms when the Cretic was resolved: thus *Cómpositióni, Éxcommunicà-tiónem, Virtútis operátio*. The medieval theorists treated these as a succession of Spondees, but there can be hardly a doubt as to their proper analysis. Again the Cursus Velox might be extended by a syllable, *Flétibus sùpplicántium,*

which coincides with an accepted metrical type
(Zielinski's Form 4). Of the three anomalous
types remaining, two (*e.g. Precibus nostris, Iugiter
postulat*) differ from the Cursus only in the Caesura,
and may have survived from reminiscence of
the ancient forms when the Caesura was not
arbitrarily restricted; and the third (*Fovemur
meritis*) may possibly have arisen from a confused
application of the Molossus base to an accentual
phrase. But all these licences are rare: they
are either excrescences upon the strict Cursus,
or they are survivals which could not be suppressed.

It has been already mentioned that there
were some parts of the document which were
by common agreement exempt from rule. These
were the Protocols, the Title, Address, and
Greeting, and the Date; secondly, quotations (for
instance) from the Bible or from documents;
and thirdly, the enumeration of properties granted
or confirmed. Nor were the rules ever completely
carried out except with regard to the terminations.
As for the beginning and middle of a sentence
I have said that little was done more than to
lay down general directions; and even these
were not consistently observed. The law against
consecutive Dactyls, for example, was often
violated.

In the twelfth century the regularity of the
rhythm of Papal Bulls increases from pontificate
to pontificate. Under Innocent III the system,
like everything else in the Papal administration,

reaches its highest point of perfection so far as
Letters are concerned. But in Privileges we
still find such terminations as *Apostolice sédis
auctoritáte, Pax Domini nostri Ihesu Christi*, even
aliena fiat. The Cursus was in fact more slowly
introduced into the more solemn documents than
it was into Letters. Probably the notaries were
reluctant to alter the traditional forms of Privileges,
all the more since the beneficiaries would not
welcome a document the style of which did
not accord with what they had been in the habit
of seeing. Besides, it was the Letters which
gave most free play to originality of composition,
so that in them the new rules would naturally
first find expression. It has indeed been supposed
that the reason for this distinction lay in the
fact that the Cursus could be recognized at once
as the special product of the Papal Chancery:
it was a safeguard which was desirable for Letters which had not the protection of the grand
dating with the Monogram and Rota and the
other conspicuous marks of Privileges; whereas
Privileges were sufficiently protected by the so-
lemnity of their external aspect. But this explanation will not serve, for the Cursus quickly
passed into the schools of Western Europe, and
there were writers everywhere who were able
and ready to apply its rules. It cannot have
served long as the special *cachet* of Papal
documents. I believe the true reason why
Privileges yielded less promptly to the reformed system is that which I have just
indicated, that people liked to have their title-

deeds drawn up in a form to which they were accustomed[1].

Writers on Dictamen in the thirteenth century attempted to construct precise rules as to choices of terminations appropriate for the several divisions of the sentence, for the comma and the period, the half-close and the full close. There was a general agreement that the sentence should end with the Cursus Velox; but some writers laid down that the Planus and Tardus should alternate in the course of the phrase, while others considered the Tardus suitable for the smallest pauses (as of a comma), and the Planus for the half-close, or colon[2]. It will not, however, be found that these elaborations of the system were ever regularly carried out in practice. The Cursus Velox indeed formed the normal termination of the sentence, but it also occupied a place, nearly as frequently as the others, in the middle; and while a sense for variety recommended that the same cadences should not be used consecutively, and much pains were taken that documents setting forth important definitions or decisions should be composed with the utmost attention to the literary canons of the age, it was deemed sufficient in ordinary business letters to see that the plain rules of the Cursus were not violated without paying regard to the further refinements of its

---

[1] Since this lecture was completed I have had the pleasure of reading Mr Clark's admirably lucid survey of the metrical and accentual Cursus contained in his lecture on Prose Rhythm in English (1913).

[2] See Valois, pp. 194 f.

use. I give a specimen of such a letter in a mandate of Innocent III making an appointment[1], in which I have indicated the accents and have noted the type of Cursus by the letters P, T, and V in the margin.

Inter omnes munitiónes et cástra	P
quae Romana ténet ecclésia,	T
munitionem et castrum Montis Fiasconis non solum inténdit	P
sed cúpit	
et providéntius gùbernári	V
et studiósius cùstodíri.	V
Cum ergo de tuae fídei pùritáte	V
indubitam fidúciam hàbeámus,	V
et de tuae discretiónis indústria	T
notitiam gerámus expértam,	P
custodiam et gubernationem ipsius munitiónis et cástri	P
tibi quandiu nobis aut successoribus nóstris placúerit	T
tanquam fideli et vassalio nostro dúximus còmmitténdum:	V
Per apostolica scrípta mandántes,	P
quatenus, sicut charam habes gratiam divínam et nóstram,	P
munitionem ípsam et cástrum	P
cum omni diligéntia èt cautéla	V
custódias èt gubérnes,	V
adhibens universa quae fúerint nècessária, (*Form* 4)	V
ita ut de contingentibus níhil omíttas.	P
Nos enim dilecto filio B. castellano Montis Fiasconis per	P
apostolica scrípta mandámus,	
ut palatium cum omnibus quae sunt in éo resígnet,	P
et serviéntibus ùnivérsis	V
ut tibi reverénter inténdant;	P
consulibus etiam atque populo quod tibi tanquam suo respón-	V
deant càstelláno	

[1] Reg. VI. 105, 30 June 1203.

V.

Our survey of the changes through which the Papal Chancery passed and of the characteristics of its productions has now advanced to two different points of time. I began with the history of the College of Notaries, and described the general structure of Papal documents and the modes by which the earlier specimens of them have been transmitted. This brought me down to the pontificate of Hadrian I and the reign of Charles the Great, and ended the First Period of the history. Next I examined the forms of documents during the two centuries and a half of transition, extending to the accession of Leo IX and making up the Second Period, a time in which there exist a fairly large number of documents preserved in originals. Then I resumed the history of the Chancery from the time of Hadrian I, but I carried it on seventy-five years beyond the election of Leo IX, because, though his pontificate marks a clear line of division so far as the forms of documents are concerned, and though it introduced important foreign elements into the Chancery, yet the policy which he instituted was such as his immediate successors were unable to maintain consistently, and it was not until the early part of the twelfth century that the old local elements in the Chancery were finally excluded. But by continuing my account down to Calixtus II I passed beyond the time at which the style of composition of Papal documents was reformed, and it seemed therefore best to introduce at that stage a description of the Cursus Curiae Romanae.

Thus the history of the Chancery has reached 1124; the employment of the medieval Cursus begins in 1088; while I have left the forms of the documents lagging behind in 1049. This irregularity, which I confess, was not unintentional. I wished to vary the subjects with which I had to deal, and it was impossible to make a sharp dividing line for each of them at the year 1049. I now go back to that year and proceed to consider the forms which documents assumed after the accession of Leo IX, the Third Period in the diplomatic history of the Roman Chancery[1].

From an external point of view the great features brought into the system by Leo IX were

---

[1] As the subject involves the consideration of a large number of small details, many of which I am obliged to leave unnoticed, I may refer to the fuller discussion of them given by F. Kaltenbrunner, Bemerkungen über die äusseren Merkmale der Pulsturkunden des 12. Jahrhunderts, in Mittheilungen, i. (1880) 373–410, and by W. Diekamp, Zum päpstlichen Urkundenwesen des xi., xii., und der ersten Hälfte des xiii. Jahrhunderts, in Mittheilungen, iii. (1882), 565–626. In reviewing my account I have derived assistance from Dr von Pflugk-Harttung's work on Die Bullen der Päpste, 1901, which is in fact a commentary on his huge collection of Specimina. While the author's proposals for the classification of the documents are pedantic and his hypotheses often fanciful, it is right to acknowledge his great industry in the accumulation of facts, his accurate palaeographical observation, and his conscientious record of details.

the abolition of the *Bene Valete* written at length
and the substitution of a Monogram, and the
introduction of the Rota to match it on the left-
hand side of the lower part of the document.
These characteristics are only found on Privileges,
a form of document which henceforward is conspicuously distinguished from the less imposing
Letter. The distinction between these two types,
and the establishment of their nomenclature, were
first plainly laid down by that great scholar
Léopold Delisle[1], to whom the study of Papal
diplomatic owes perhaps as much—and it is
difficult to say more—as any other branch of
medieval criticism. Previous writers had spoken
obscurely of Great and Little Bulls, without
clearly bringing out their fundamental difference
in external form and indeed in purpose. The
terms Privilege and Letter precisely indicate this
distinction. The Privilege is as a rule the instrument of the grant or confirmation of rights of
property and jurisdiction to churches and religious
houses. It was a title-deed, to be preserved in a
muniment chest and produced on solemn occasions.
Therefore it was drawn up on a great skin of
parchment and made imposing by means of
elaborate formulae and attestations and certificates
of authenticity. Letters, on the other hand, were
down to the middle of the fifteenth century the
regular vehicle of the Popes' official correspondence
whether on spiritual or political subjects. They
form a class of much greater historical and legal

[1] Mémoire sur les Actes d'Innocent III, in the Bibliothèque
de l'École des Chartes, 4th series, iv. (1858), 16–22.

importance than Privileges. Decretals, encyclical letters, bulls defining the Pope's authority or denouncing alleged invasions of it, equally with commissions, licences, and other documents of every-day business, all belong to the form of Letters.

For the present I limit myself to the Privilege, and begin by describing the Rota and Monogram. These were the first public marks of Leo's activity. After his election at Rome in February 1049 he did not enter the Lateran Palace until 13 April, and on the 22nd the Rota makes its appearance[1]. This is an elaboration of the Cross which preceded the *Bene Valete*; but now it is surrounded by two concentric circles. At first between the limbs of the Cross we read simply the Pope's name.

$$\begin{array}{c|c} \text{L} & \text{E} \\ \hline \text{O} & \text{P} \end{array}$$

But this arrangement was not applicable to the names chosen by Leo IX's successors, and a number of new forms were employed. In the following lists the names of Antipopes are placed within brackets[2].

Victor II:
$$\begin{array}{c|c} \overline{\text{IHS}} & \overline{\text{XPS}} \\ \hline \text{PETRUS} & \text{PAULUS} \end{array}$$

Stephen IX:
$$\begin{array}{c|c} \text{ᴀ} & \text{ω} \\ \hline \overline{\text{IC}} & \overline{\text{XC}} \end{array}$$

[1] Montfaucon, Diarium Italicum, pp. 325 ff., 1702 [Jaffé, Reg. 4165]. Cf. Spec. 18.

[2] The writing on both parts of the Rota varies between capitals and minuscules. As I do not attempt to give facsimiles I have used capitals throughout and have extended some of the contractions. I have also disregarded variations in spelling.

Benedict X:
$$\frac{\text{PAX} \mid \text{OMNIBUS}}{\overline{\text{XPI}} \mid \text{FIDELIBUS}}$$

Nicholas II:
$$\frac{\overline{\text{XPC}} \mid \text{VINCIT}}{\text{PETRUS} \mid \text{PAULUS}}$$

Alexander II:
$$\frac{\text{MAGNUS} \mid \text{DNS NR}}{\text{ET MAGNA} \mid \text{VIRTUS EIVS}}$$

Gregory VII:
$$\frac{\text{MISERATIONES} \mid \text{TUE DNE}}{\text{SUPER OMNIA} \mid \text{OPERA TUA}}$$

[Clement III:
$$\frac{\overline{\text{IHC}} \mid \overline{\text{XC}}}{\overline{\text{DNS}} \mid \text{NR}}$$

with CONFIRMA HOC DEUS QUOD OPERATUS ES IN NOBIS written on the arms of the Cross.]

Urban II:
$$\frac{\begin{array}{c}\overline{\text{SCS}} \\ \text{PETRUS}\end{array} \mid \begin{array}{c}\overline{\text{SCS}} \\ \text{PAULUS}\end{array}}{\begin{array}{c}\text{UR} \\ \overline{\text{PP}}\end{array} \mid \begin{array}{c}\text{BANUS} \\ \text{II}\end{array}}$$

The style adopted by Urban II became the accepted one. It had the advantage of simplicity; and besides it reproduced the legend on the two sides of the leaden *bulla* attached to the document, and thus formed a link between the Privilege and the seal which authenticated it.

Round the circumference, between the two circles, is written the Device. This is almost always a text from the Bible which was adopted once for all by each Pope and retained throughout his pontificate. The following is a list of the Devices found from their introduction to the time of Innocent III[1].

Leo IX: MISERICORDIA DOMINI PLENA EST TERRA.

Victor II: VICTORIS ·II· SANCTAE ROMANAE ET APOSTOLICAE SEDIS PAPAE[2].

Stephen IX: IPSE EST PAX NOSTRA.

Benedict X: DOMNI BENEDICTI DECIMI PAPAE.

Nicholas II: CONFIRMA HOC DEUS QUOD OPERATUS ES IN NOBIS.

Alexander II: i. EXALTAVIT ME DEUS IN VIRTUTE BRACHII SUI.

                 ii. DEUS NOSTER REFUGIUM ET VIRTUS[3].

Gregory VII: (No device round the circle).

[Clement III: i. DOMINI EST TERRA ET PLENITUDO EIUS.

                 ii. VERBO DOMINI CAELI FIRMATI SUNT.]

Victor III: (No original preserved).

Urban II: i. BENEDICTUS DEUS ET PATER DOMINI NOSTRI IESU CHRISTI (sometimes followed by AMEN).

                 ii. LEGIMUS · FIRMAVIMUS[4].

[1] I have taken almost all the Devices from Dr von Pflugk-Harttung's Specimina, and have completed the series from the data supplied by Jaffé at the beginning of each pontificate. The list given in Cardinal Pitra's Analecta novissima Spicilegii Solesmensis, i. 310–312 (1885), is inaccurately drawn up; it does not distinguish between the texts written round the Rota and those in the centre and even includes one found only on the *bulla*. Antipopes of whose Devices I have found no examples are omitted.

[2] An alternative form is VICTORIS PRIME SEDIS EPISCOPI ET UNIVERSALIS PAPAE SECUNDI.

[3] A document of 15 May 1066 contains both these devices, the second written between the circles, the first outside them. Spec. 39 (1). The second text is sometimes miswritten, with DEI for DEUS and NOSTRUM for NOSTER.

[4] This inscription (Spec. 48 [4]) or LEGIMUS · AMEN · FIRMAVIMUS · AMEN (Spec. 48 [2 and 3]) is found occasionally, from October 1096 onwards. In a Privilege for St Basle near Rheims Urban wrote LEGIMUS · FIRMAVIMUS · SANCTE · BASOLE (Spec. 48 [1]).

Paschal II:	VERBO DOMINI CELI FIRMATI SUNT.
Gelasius II:	(No specimen of a solemn Privilege[1]).
Calixtus II:	FIRMAMENTUM EST DOMINUS TIMENTIBUS EUM.
Honorius II:	OCULI DOMINI SUPER IUSTOS.
Innocent II:	ADIUVA NOS DEUS SALUTARIS NOSTER.
[Anacletus II:	DOMINUS FORTITUDO PLEBIS SUE.]
Celestine II:	FIAT PAX IN VIRTUTE TUA ET HABUNDANTIA IN TURRIBUS TUIS.
Lucius II:	OSTENDE NOBIS DOMINE MISERICORDIAM TUAM.
Eugenius III:	FAC MECUM DOMINE SIGNUM IN BONUM.
Anastasius IV:	CUSTODI ME DOMINE UT PUPILLA OCULI.
Hadrian IV:	OCULI MEI SEMPER AD DOMINUM.
Alexander III:	VIAS TUAS DOMINE DEMONSTRA MICHI.
[Victor IV:	TU ES GLORIA MEA TU ES SUSCEPTOR MEUS TU EXALTAS CAPUT MEUM DOMINE.]
[Paschal III:	ADIUTOR MEUS ESTO DOMINE! NE DERELINQUAS ME.]
[Calixtus III:	CONSERVA ME DOMINE QUONIAM SPERAVI IN TE[2].]
Lucius III:	ADIUVA NOS DEUS SALUTARIS NOSTER.
Urban III:	AD TE DOMINE LEVAVI ANIMAM MEAM.
Gregory VIII:	DIRIGE ME DOMINE IN VERITATE TUA.
Clement III:	DOCE ME DOMINE FACERE VOLUNTATEM TUAM.
Celestine III:	PERFICE GRESSUS MEOS IN SEMITIS TUIS.
Innocent III:	FAC MECUM DOMINE SIGNUM IN BONUM.

Thus in a century and a half the principle that the Device should contain a text continued almost unbroken. Shortly after its introduction indeed Victor II and Benedict X (if he be reckoned a Pope) preferred to inscribe their title preceded by a small Cross, which was sometimes repeated at intervals more than once; but the form once

---

[1] Pflugk-Harttung, Die Bullen der Päpste, p. 263.

[2] So in Spec. 95, from Psalm xv. [XVI.] i; in Spec. 94 (3) the last three words are transposed.

chosen was maintained unaltered by all the acknowledged Popes except Alexander II and
Urban II. The change made by the latter substituted for the Device what was in effect an
additional confirmation[1]. But Urban's example
was not followed by subsequent Popes. It will
be observed that, while Lucius III adopted the
Device of Innocent II, and Innocent III that of
Eugenius III, every other Pope invented a text
for himself[2].

As the Rota was an amplified Cross, so conversely the Monogram which stands on the right
hand was a compressed *Bene Valete*. It is like
other Monograms such as had long been used by
the Emperors. But their monogram contained
the letters of the Emperor's name, while that of
the Pope represented the final Greeting. The
letters of the words are there, but the same letters
have to be used more than once. The Monogram
varies in size: sometimes it is nearly four inches
high. Closely associated with it is the Comma
placed on its right. But this was not an invention
of Leo IX; it is found a good deal earlier. It has
been explained as a mark of punctuation[3]; but
its place is often taken by strokes which look like
an abbreviation of *Subscripsi*[4]. Possibly the

[1] Pflugk-Harttung, Die Bullen der Päpste, p. 223.

[2] Later Popes were less ingenious. Honorius III and Gregory X
borrowed the Device of Celestine III; Gregory IX, Urban IV, and
Innocent VI that of Eugenius III and Innocent III; Clement IV
and Innocent V that of Hadrian IV; and Eugenius IV actually
that of the Antipope Paschal III: see Pitra, pp. 311 f.

[3] Pflugk-Harttung, in Mittheilungen, v. (1884) 434; Giry,
Manuel de Diplomatique, p. 620; cf. p. 597.

[4] *Ibid.*, p. 671.

Comma is a corruption or ornamental perversion of this abbreviated *Subscripsi*, for it takes the place of what unmistakeably stands for *Subscripsi*. At the time when the *Bene Valete* was written in full it was usually preceded and followed by a Cross. Then under Benedict VIII the second Cross is replaced by a very distinct · ∫∫ ·[1]; and under his successor John XIX this · ∫∫ · becomes a complex of commas (; ⁱ ,)[2]. Under Clement II it may be reduced to a single comma[3], or it may be three composite signs, one above the other (⋛)[4]; but relics of a long ∫ may still be found[5]. The Comma had become conventional, and probably its origin was forgotten. What Leo IX did was to magnify it enormously, so that it becomes more than half as tall as the Monogram itself (∴ ᴐ)[6]. But it did not survive long. Under Stephen IX and again under Nicholas II its place was taken by a little rosette or quatrefoil[7]. Nor was it always written, and when it does appear there are usually signs of a long ∫[8] which seems to be a reminiscence of the *Subscripsi*. I do not think that the Comma is found after Gregory VII. A brief interval follows, and then the Comma is finally superseded by the Pope's Subscription in full[9].

The great innovation made by Leo IX was a

---

[1] Spec. 10, 11. [2] *Ibid.* 12.
[3] *Ibid.* 14 (1). [4] *Ibid.* 14 (2), 16.
[5] *Ibid.* 15. [6] *Ibid.* 17 (2).
[7] *Ibid.* 17; Kehr, Scrinium et Palatium, in Mittheilungen, Suppl. vol. vi. 90.
[8] Spec. 30, 35 (4). [9] See below, p. 109.

pictorial one. The Rota and Monogram and the exaggerated Comma stand out conspicuously from the rest of the document. But Leo did not alter the formulae: *In Perpetuum* had for ages concluded the address[1]. Nor was he the inventor of the tall laterally compressed Minuscule letters in which the first line was written. That line had long been written in Capitals or Uncials of various types, and Leo employed every sort of style; while on the other hand the compressed Minuscule in the opening Protocol had made its appearance a little before his pontificate, under Clement II[2]. Apart from the Rota and Monogram, which emerge immediately after Leo's election, though they are not found quite invariably[3], the distinctive marks of the Privilege are only developed by degrees. In some Bulls of 1062 and 1063 the name of Alexander II is written in Capitals between the Rota and the Monogram[4]; and exceptionally under Victor II and Nicholas II[5] we may find witnesses. These witnesses are of interest, because they lead us to the question of the autograph element in the document. A Bull of Victor II for Monte Cassino, June 1057, is not only written throughout by the hand of Humbert, Cardinal

---

[1] As an instance of the confusion which prevailed in the Chancery of Alexander II I note a document with some of the features of a Privilege which has only the Pope's name in Capitals and in which the Address is followed by the epistolary Greeting: Spec. 102 (1) [Jaffé, Reg. 4490].

[2] Spec. 16.

[3] See Kehr, Scrinium et Palatium, p. 86, note 4.

[4] See three examples in Spec. 31.

Spec. 29 (2), 30 (4).

Bishop of Selva Candida, but is subscribed by
him and by Hildebrand, Cardinal Deacon[1]. Hildebrand's autograph as Pope appears in the Device
which he wrote in the field of his Rota[2]. Before
him there are examples of the handwriting of
Nicholas II and of Alexander II[3] in at least the
upper half of the field. Apparently this part was
reserved for completion by the highest authority
that could be obtained, if possible by the Pope himself; and sometimes its completion was omitted[4].
It was the technical Firmatio. Possibly the same
hand inserted the Cross, or at least the horizontal
bar of it. When this was finished the Device was
added[5].

The type of Privilege slowly evolved, under
the manifold changes of organization which were
made in the Chancery during the eleventh century, was not completely established until the
pontificate of Paschal II (1099–1118) when John
of Gaetà was Chancellor. Under him begins the

---

[1] Spec. 26 [Jaffé, Reg. 4368]. Humbert's handwriting will
also be found in the Data of all the Privileges of Stephen IX and
in most of those of Nicholas II of which the originals are preserved. See Kehr, Diplomatische Miszellen, III., in Nachrichten
von der Königlichen Gesellschaft der Wissenschaften zu Göttingen,
Philol.-hist. Klasse, 1900, pp. 104 f.

[2] Four examples will be found in Spec. 41. These are of
18 January 1074 [Jaffé, Reg. 4818], 7 March 1074 [n. 4940],
24 March 1074 [n. 4945], and 4 April 1080 [n. 5160].

[3] See Pflugk-Harttung, Die Bullen der Päpste, pp. 184,
195 ff.

[4] Thus Nicholas II, 25 April 1061: Spec. 28 (2).

[5] This at least was the rule later, and an examination of
the ink leads to the opinion that it prevailed from the time
of Calixtus II: see Kaltenbrunner, in Mittheilungen, i. 383;
Diekamp, *ibid.*, iii. 574 ff. But it may have been observed
earlier: see above, p. 74 note 3.

Subscription of the Pope[1] written at length between the Rota and the Monogram.

Ego Paschalis Catholicę Ecclesie Episcopus ſſ.

We may now expect to find the following features in the document[2].

1. The opening Protocol is written in laterally compressed Minuscules, the Title and Address being terminated by *In Perpetuum*.

2. The Text ends with one or more Amens.

3. There are the Rota and the Monogram.

4. Between them are the Subscriptions of the Pope and of some Cardinals, the latter each preceded by a Cross[3]; if there are many they are arranged in three columns, the Bishops in the middle and the Priests and Deacons to left and right[4].

5. The Scriptum and the Datum may both appear; but the former is dying out and is not found after 1124[5]. Of the officers concerned with these elements I have already treated[6]. After Calixtus II the Chancellor no longer writes the

---

[1] This is said to be only partly autograph. Diekamp thinks that Hadrian IV wrote the *Ego* and Alexander III and his successors only the *E*; *ibid.*, pp. 578 f.

[2] See for an instance Spec. 64.

[3] According to Kaltenbrunner and Diekamp, after the document had received the Pope's Subscription and been adorned with the Rota and Monogram, it was circulated among the Cardinals, who each wrote a Cross and began the Subscription, but left it to be finished by a clerk; *ubi supra*, i. 387, iii. 580–587.

[4] Spec. 74 (1).

[5] See above, p. 74. It has been suggested that it was the omission of the Scriptum which led to the elaboration and the multiplication of the Amens by way of compensation. An example of the Scriptum in 1122 is in Spec. 59.

[6] Above, pp. 64–75.

whole Datum, but inserts, or occasionally omits to insert, his name in a gap left open for it[1]. The Datum was from the time of Victor II, but not always, furnished with the name of the place where the document was dated: *Datum in castro Casino*[2] or the like.

The date of time requires special attention, for towards the end of the eleventh century both the reckoning of the Christian year and of the Indiction became subject to variation[3]. Down to Urban II the former was regularly understood to begin with Christmas. The only exception was during a fortnight in 1060, when Nicholas II was at Florence or in its immediate neighbourhood from 8 to 20 January and employed the *calculus Florentinus* beginning on the 25th March after the commencement of our calendar year. But with Urban II uniformity ceases. He made use of the Florentine computation and of that of Pisa, which began the year twelve months earlier[4], alternatively with the year of the Nativity; and this chronological laxity persisted until the death of Innocent II[5]. With Eugenius III the *calculus Florentinus* became the established style[6].

Moreover, after Gregory VII the old Greek Indiction beginning on 1 September no longer always prevailed: the Indiction of 24 September

---

[1] Spec. 64, 74; cf. 80.   [2] Stephen IX, 1057: Spec. 27.

[3] Compare above, pp. 49 f.

[4] The Pisan style is found especially in documents of 1095 and 1096.

[5] Calixtus II does not seem to have favoured the Florentine reckoning.

[6] But even later Alexander III sometimes began the year at Christmas.

known as that of Bede, and the so-called Roman
Indiction of Christmas, forced their way in. The
first of these is seldom found in the documents of
Urban II, who generally employed the other two;
under his successors on the contrary, down to
and including Eugenius III, no example of the
Bedan style has been noticed, the Greek and the
Roman Indictions being the only reckonings used.
Then under Anastasius IV and Hadrian IV the
Roman Indiction prevails exclusively. Finally,
Alexander III, though he uses this sometimes,
generally adopts the Indiction of Bede. Thus
the practice of Alexander III, which continued
in the Papal Chancery down to modern times,
represented in both points the rule observed at
Florence, where the year began on 25 March of
our calendar year and the Indiction on the preceding 24 September[1].

The form of Solemn Privilege, or Great Bull,
with its manifold elaboration, was found inconvenient for use on all occasions, and a simplified
type was constructed early in the twelfth century.
Indeed, before this time there are. examples of
the more pictorial features of the Privilege being

[1] I take these chronological statements from the data supplied
by Jaffé at the beginning of the Regesta of the several Popes.
To verify them would involve the examination of several thousand
documents and the recalculation of every date in them. But
I should add that in some particulars Jaffé's results have not
always been accepted. Thus Dr H. Grotefend asserts that
Urban II used only the Indiction of Bede, and that Eugenius III
(from 1147) and his successors employed all three systems:
Zeitrechnung des Deutschen Mittelalters und der Neuzeit, i. 93 *b*,
1891.

dispensed with. It is possible that John of Gaetà, with his long experience as Chancellor, designed, when he became Pope, as Gelasius II, in 1118, to abolish once for all the Rota and Monogram, and in their place to write at the foot of the document his autograph Subscription and Device[1]:

Ego Gelasius ecclesię catholicę episcopus ſſ. Signum manus meę. Deus in loco sancto suo[2].

But if this was his intention, it was not carried out by his successors. They might omit the Rota and Monogram, but they hardly ever wrote the Device after their subscription[3]. What they did was to create—what had been used occasionally before[4]—the type of the Simple Privilege, which is marked not only by the absence of the Rota and Monogram but also by the substitution of the epistolary Greeting, *Salutem et apostolicam benedictionem*, for the majestic *In Perpetuum*. But for these two changes the characteristics of the Privilege are retained: the document still begins with tall Minuscules; it usually bears the Subscriptions of Pope[5] and Cardinals; and above all there is the full Chancery Date, *Datum per manum Iohannis cancellarii*, or the like. Intermediate varieties may for a time be found, and the fixed form of the Simple Privilege is not established until the pontificate of Innocent II (1130–1143).

[1] Cf. Pflugk-Harttung, Die Bullen der Päpste, p. 93.

[2] Spec. 103.

[3] One instance exists under Innocent II, 5 June 1133: Spec. 105.

[4] Thus, by Urban II: Spec. 102.

[5] To make up for the absence of the Rota Calixtus II prefixed ℟ to his name, and his successors a Cross.

Before that time a Simple Privilege may look very much like a Letter, and one may be deceived by the Greeting, *Salutem et apostolicam benedictionem*; but if it has the full Chancery date, as 'Given at the Lateran by the hand of' so and so, or at all events a date written on a line by itself separated from the text, it is a Privilege; if the words 'Given at the Lateran,' at such a date, immediately follow the text, it is a Letter. The Simple Privilege was in fact a modification of the form of the Solemn Privilege which adopted some of the features of the Letter. It died out under Innocent III when it had been found possible to effect the same object by a development of the Letter[1].

The type of the Letter had been settled long before the Simple Privilege came into existence, and for the sake of clearness it will be best to leave this intermediate form out of our minds, and to contrast the Letter with the Solemn Privilege. The distinction in appearance and in structure is a broad one. To begin with, the Letter is a much smaller document. It has no Rota or Monogram, no Subscriptions, no statement about the writing or the official dating. There is a Greeting after the Address, and the Text of the document is directly followed, on the same line if there is room, by a simple record of the place, day, and month[2]. But this precise method of dating did not come in until the time of Urban II. The Indiction may sometimes be added until Calixtus II, but

---

[1] See Kaltenbrunner, in Mittheilungen, i. 403 f.
[2] Spec. 110.

it was omitted by his successor Honorius II. This remained the rule, except during the short pontificate of Gregory VIII (1187–1188) and the beginning of that of Clement III, until 11 February 1188 when the Pontifical year, *pontificatus nostri anno primo* (or the like), was introduced into Letters. This Pontifical year came to rank as the most important element in the date. It was never abbreviated, but always written out at length[1]. These details are of service in helping us to ascribe to the right Pope Letters of which we do not possess the originals, as Popes of the same name were many and their number was never given except on their seals. Delisle has shown how they enable us to distinguish between the Letters of Innocent II, Innocent III, and Innocent IV. Moreover, the date of place will often of itself settle the proper attribution. By these means also we are furnished with a *prima facie* argument against the genuineness of Letters in which a form inconsistent with the period makes its appearance[2].

During the earlier part of the period very few Letters are preserved in originals. We have three of Alexander II and two of Gregory VII. They do not become abundant until the time of Innocent II and Eugenius III. They are written on small oblong pieces of parchment, and space is economized in every possible way. This is a great mark of distinction from the form of the Privilege, in which considerations of space were disregarded.

---

[1] See Delisle, Mémoire, pp. 59 f.

[2] *Ibid.*, pp. 60–67.

In the earlier time the Pope's name was indicated only by his initial; it was not until Innocent II that it was usually written out in full. The Text commonly consisted only of a Statement of the Case and an Enacting Clause, a Narratio and a Dispositio; but in the twelfth century, for reasons which will be explained immediately, certain kinds of Letters came to appropriate some of the features of Privileges.

Letters were in the first place the instruments of the record of the Pope's administrative and judicial acts: they contained his orders and in a large proportion of cases may be described as Mandates. But an order to redress a grievance, a commission to enquire into alleged irregularities, and the like deal with an affair of the moment, and when the command has been executed the purpose of the document is accomplished. In the twelfth century the scope of the Letter was extended and it began to deal with matters which had previously formed the subject of Privileges; that is to say, it came to confer permanent rights. There thus arose two varieties of Letters, which while preserving a common type were distinguished not only in their purport but also in their mode of writing and in the attachment of the leaden *bulla*. These two classes are Tituli or Litterae de Gratia, and Mandamenta or Litterae de Iustitia. According to their contents the one may be called Licences or Indults, the other Mandates or Commissions. In the former the seal was attached by a silk cord, in the latter by a string of hemp; and so they were called *litterae cum filo serico* and *litterae cum filo canapis.* In earlier times Letters, like Privileges, had silk ties more commonly than string: now, grace is uniformly associated with the softer material, justice with the rougher[1]. Another reason for the choice of string for Mandates was very likely that these were not intended to be preserved after their order had been carried out, so that it was unnecessary to go to the expense of silk. These distinctions were developed by degrees. The special use of silk and hemp was first adopted by Innocent II (1130–1143), but the distinction was not perhaps inflexibly observed until the middle of the thirteenth century. The employment of an elaborate and ornamental calligraphy for Tituli appears under Lucius II (1144–1145).

I shall now say something of these two classes of Letters separately. Letters of Grace or Tituli are documents by which the Pope grants or confirms rights, confers benefices, promulgates statutes or decrees, or decides causes. Their characteristic sentences open with *Auctoritate praesentium indulgemus* or *inhibemus, Auctoritate apostolica confirmamus, Auctoritate sedis apostolicae confirmamus,* or the like. They are grants, confirmations, licences, indults, decrees, of many sorts. Frequently they fulfil the same purpose which had in earlier times been effected by the Privilege, and from the Privilege they adopt three elements, though these are not necessarily present: the

---

[1] This distinction was first pointed out by Delisle, Mémoire, pp. 19 f. It may be said to have been regularly observed, for the few exceptions which have been noticed can be accounted for by special circumstances.

Preamble or Arenga, and the Final Clauses *Nulli ergo* and *Si quis autem.* These are taken over without alteration into the Letter of Grace. The Text is more formal than that of the Mandate, and the writing is more decorative, because the document was intended to be preserved. And thus, after a period of fluctuating forms, it came to be laid down that the Pope's name must be written in elongated letters like the first line of a Privilege, the initial letter being raised higher with open spaces within it and sometimes floriations. The Address must begin with a large Majuscule initial. Marks of abbreviation are made with an ornamental sign (8 or 7), and what is most conspicuous *ct* and *st* are written with a space between them and a horizontal ligature resembling the ɾt still used in certain types. These features are borrowed from the Privilege.

As distinguished from Tituli, Letters of Justice or Mandates convey the Pope's administrative orders, by injunction or prohibition or by the appointment of commissioners to carry out some definite work; they include also the mass of his official correspondence on matters of all sorts, both political (*Litterae secretae*) and administrative (*Litterae de Curia*) as they came in time to be distinguished. They were produced in great numbers, and practical considerations demanded that they should be as flexible and as little encumbered by formulae as they could be. They may read like the ordinary letters of other churchmen, but when they declare the Pope's command they usually contain such words as *Per apostolica scripta* or

Praecipiendo mandamus. The Address often omits the name of the dignitary to whom the mandate was sent and gives instead two full points. This was done not from ignorance of the name but in order to secure that the order should be carried out in the case of another dignitary having been appointed after the document was issued. As for the writing, when the type was fully settled, only the initial letter of the Pope's name was written in Majuscule. In like manner the first word in the Address began with a plain Majuscule initial. Signs of abbreviation are simple and without ornamentation[1].

The immense increase in the Pope's business in the twelfth century made it impossible that he should personally read and examine every document for the issue of which he made himself responsible. If it was a Letter of a normal pattern, a Licence, Dispensation, or the like, it was sufficient that he should satisfy himself that it carried out his intention: it was called a Letter *in forma communi* or *sub forma communi*, and its terms were left to the Chancery officials. But if it contained new or disputable matter, a definition of law or a statement of policy, it was kept back for the Pope to hear it read through and approve it. Such documents were called *Litterae legendae*. By the end of the thirteenth century these two categories

---

[1] For these rules see below, Appendix v. There are good facsimiles, on a reduced scale, of Mandates of Innocent II (1138), Eugenius III (1145), and Innocent IV (1254), in F. Steffens' Lateinische Paläographie (1903–1906), plates lxvii, lxxv. The last may be compared with a Letter of Grace of Boniface VIII (1299) on the same plate.

were distinguished by the form of the Capital initial which followed the Greeting[1].

All Papal documents, whether Privileges or Letters, were authenticated by the *bulla* or leaden seal[2], which was attached by a string of silk or hemp. We have seen how these two materials came to be appropriated to special types of Letters. The seal itself, which is of high antiquity, contained simply the Pope's name in the genitive, LEONIS PAPAE, with some decoration; thus Leo IX inserted his number in the middle, $\frac{IIII}{V}$. His successors attempted more ornamental forms, sometimes with inscriptions round the circumference. Thus Victor II and Nicholas II showed the bust of St Peter and a hand delivering to him a key, with a legend round it, in the one case + TU PRO ME NAVEM LIQUISTI SUSCIPE CLAVEM, in the other + TIBI PETRE DABO CLAVES REGNI CELORUM; and the counter-seal of Victor bore a view of a church and that of Nicholas the design of a gate of Rome, surmounted by the words AUREA ROMA, and encircled by the Pope's name, VICTORIS PAPAE II, SECUNDI NICOLAI PAPE[3]. But before long a fixed pattern was laid down by

---

[1] See Delisle, Mémoire, pp. 21 f.

[2] No example of a golden *bulla* is known in the Middle Ages, but the use of such a material is attested in the thirteenth century. See Bresslau, i. 939 note 5 (1st ed.). On two occasions, in times of difficulty, Gregory VII dispensed with his leaden *bulla* lest it should be seized and attached to a forged document: Reg. VIII. 40, Epist. Collect. XI (Monum. Greg., ed. Jaffé, pp. 492, 568). Probably on these occasions he made use of a wax seal.

[3] Spec. 131 (7, 8).

Urban II, who placed his name in the nominative on the seal, and the names of the Apostles with a Cross on the counterseal[1]

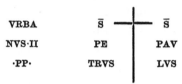

VRBA	s̄	s̄
NVS·II	PE	PAV
·PP·	TRVS	LVS

The Apostles' heads, which had appeared on Gregory VII's seal, were restored by Paschal II, a Cross was inserted between them, and the letters S. PA. S. PE. written above; and this type, with such modifications of detail as approved themselves to the taste of the designer, persisted thenceforward unchanged[2]. In course of time a fixed number of dots were required to surround the circumference, to mark off the heads from the space occupied by the Cross, and to fill in the hair and beard of St Peter; and as these dots were increased or diminished in different pontificates, to count them furnished a test of genuineness[3].

The seal was attached as a rule by means of a string looped through holes[4] in the fold of parchment at the foot of the document. After the parchment was folded, the ends of the string might be passed round it and tied together, so

[1] Consequently the heads did not suffer so much from the stroke of the hammer as the obverse did, and one die of the counterseal might remain in use for nearly seventy years (1186–1252). See Diekamp, in Mittheilungen, iii. 609, 613–626.

[2] See Spec. 130–138.

[3] On the Demi-Bull see below, Appendix VII.

[4] From the time of Innocent II, regularly two holes; previously the number had varied: see Kaltenbrunner, in Mittheilungen, i. 409; Diekamp, pp. 611 f.

as to secure it in transmission [1]. If it was desired
to prevent the Letter being read without cutting
the string, a different method was employed, in
which the Letter was first folded across and then
downwards more than once, two holes were
pierced in the joined edges at the side of the
document, the hemp string was passed through
the multiple surfaces of the parchment, and finally
the seal was imposed. By this means it was
impossible to see any of the writing until the seal
had been detached either by cutting the string or
ripping open the parchment. Such documents
were called Letters Close (*litterae clausae*) but
specimens of them are extremely rare. The first
known example occurs as early as the time of
Calixtus II [2], and the system of ' closing' Letters
was in full operation under Innocent III [3].

The system of which I have indicated the
outlines was the product of a century and a half
of trained experience. On the one hand, there

[1] See below, Appendix VII.

[2] This document (Jaffé, Reg. 6855) is dated 25 June 1120 and
is preserved in the Royal Archives at Munich. It is printed by
U. Robert, Le Bullaire du Pape Calixte II, i. (1891), 266, n. 179.
The manner in which it is sealed is figured in Monsignor P. M.
Baumgarten's Aus Kanzlei und Kammer (1907), p. 195. Two
Letters Close of Alexander III (1162 and 1164) at Barcelona are
described with illustrations by M. E. Martin-Chabot in Mélanges
d'Archéologie et d'Histoire, xxiv. (1904), 65–74. Another specimen
of Alexander III is reproduced in Monum. Graphica medii Aevi,
ix. 4.

[3] Cf. Delisle, pp. 20 f. Innocent mentions, evidently by way
of distinction, *litterae patentes*: Reg. VI. 165. It is interesting to
notice the emergence of these names at the very same time as
they first appear in the English Chancery.

was a desire to make the instruments of the Pope's authority more readily accessible; hence the expensive type of Privilege was, except for rare and opulent beneficiaries, superseded first by the Simple Privilege and then by the Letter of Grace[1]. On the other hand, the more documents were multiplied and scattered abroad, the greater was the risk of forgery; therefore they were hedged round, in every point, by minute technical prescriptions. These two causes conspired with the natural tendency of a thoroughly organized office towards order and exact routine, to develop the severely regulated work of the Chancery of the beginning of the thirteenth century which is as perfect in its calligraphy as it is diplomatically without fault.

[1] A further blow at the Solemn Privilege was struck by the invention under Innocent IV of the Intermediate Bull. Its Text, Final Protocol, and Dating were essentially those of the Letter; but the first line was written in elongated characters, often with great and even magnificent elaboration. Besides this feature, it borrowed from the Solemn Privilege the *In Perpetuum* but in a modified form: the words are not always exactly the same, but the phrase most generally used was *Ad perpetuam rei memoriam* or *Ad futuram rei memoriam*.

VI.

It has been noticed in an earlier connexion that
for the interval of a hundred and seventy years
which elapsed between the death of Stephen V
and the election of Alexander II in 1061 there is
no trace in any quotation or excerpt that any
Papal Register was ever composed[1]. The fact
that all this time the Chancery was continuously
active is an argument against the supposition that
the practice of registering Papal documents was
given up[2]; and the reason why no extracts from
Registers are preserved is probably that the Letters
of the Popes of that time did not furnish materials
which were of value for the compilers of canonical
collections, and these compilers are our only
witnesses to the existence of Registers which are
no longer preserved. The Popes might issue
Privileges when required; but they were not in
a position, even if their aptitudes qualified them,
to declare rules of ecclesiastical order or judicature.
After the accession of Leo IX we find extracts
from the Registers of Alexander II[3], Urban II[4],

---

[1] Above, p. 36.   [2] See Bresslau, i. 107 f.

[3] Eighty-seven Letters are contained in the Collectio Britannica (Add. MS. 8873); see Ewald, in Neues Archiv, v. 326–352.
Most of them are printed by S. Löwenfeld, Epist. Pontif. Roman.
ined., 1885, pp. 38–58. Others are given by Cardinal Deusdedit,
IV. 95, 423, &c.

[4] Neues Archiv, v. 352–366; Löwenfeld, pp. 59–64.

and Alexander III[1]; and it is certain that the
Registers of Urban II and of several of his successors were still in existence in the thirteenth
century[2]. But, if we except a small fragment of
a Register of the Antipope Anacletus II for the
year 1130[3], only one Register remains to us.
That is the Register of Gregory VII, the solitary
survivor of the time preceding Innocent III.

This famous book claims special attention, not
only on account of the supreme importance of
Gregory's pontificate, but also because it has
during the past thirty years been the subject of
voluminous and intricate discussion[4], and it is
only within recent times that anything approaching
general agreement has been arrived at as to its
character, its composition, and its date. These
questions had been treated from critical, diplomatic, and historical points of view, but the
palaeographical examination of the manuscript
was neglected; indeed, since Wilhelm von Giesebrecht collated it in 1844, no one until lately ever
undertook its systematic study. The book, preserved in the Vatican Archives, is a quarto volume
of 258 leaves. It is arranged not as in earlier
times by Indictions, but by Pontifical years, each
beginning on 30 June. If complete, it ought to

[1] Trinity College, Cambridge, MS. R. 9. 17, printed by
Löwenfeld, pp. 149–208 (cf. Neues Archiv, x., 1885, 586 f.).

[2] Bresslau, i. 109, notes 2 and 3.

[3] A manuscript of the early part of the fourteenth century at
Monte Cassino: see Paul Ewald, in Neues Archiv, iii., 1878,
164–168.

[4] The two papers published by Father Peitz and Dr Caspar
in 1911 and 1913 extend to 436 pages, and that by Dr Blaul,
1912, dealing only with the Dictatus, adds 116 more.

contain twelve books, but in fact there are only eight, of which the first seven are markedly distinguished in a number of details from the eighth[1]. The first seven contain documents entered substantially in a continuous chronological order down to 8 May 1080. The next month was a time of disturbance, when the Pope had to withdraw to the border of Capua and an Antipope was elected. It is not therefore surprising that the eighth book should include some documents belonging to the closing weeks of the seventh Pontifical year, which it had not been possible to register at the time of their composition. But this eighth book is not merely irregular in its beginning; it goes on to include documents of the ninth and eleventh years, but passes over the tenth year entirely[2]. Moreover, the order of time is altogether confused. It would appear that, in the troubled years of the close of his pontificate, Gregory was not in a position to secure that his Register should be regularly carried on.

The number of pieces contained in the volume is reckoned at 381, but the total is really somewhat larger[3]. Still the collection is so extremely small

---

[1] In books I.–VII. the addresses are given without the formal appellatives (*dilecto in Christo filio*, and the like) which appear in originals; in book VIII. they are written out in full but the name is often merely indicated by an initial. Books I.–VII. begin the date with *Data* and state precisely the month, day, and Indiction; book VIII. has *Datum*, hardly ever mentions the Indiction, and frequently omits the month and day.

[2] The division of the book into VIII., IX., and XI., is due to a later hand.

[3] Jaffé numbers 86 pieces in book I., 77 in II., 21 in III., 28 in IV., 23 in V., 40 in VI., 28 in VII., 23 in VIII. 1–23, and 37 in VIII. 24–60;

that it was natural that it should be considered to
be not the Pope's actual Register but a volume of
excerpts made from it for some particular purpose.
This was the view maintained by Giesebrecht and
Jaffé[1], which was accepted with hardly any dissent
until a few years ago[2]. The first seven books, it
was held, and perhaps the first thirty-two documents in the eighth, formed a selection from the
original Register,—written some time before the
middle of 1081; and the remaining portion was
derived from any materials the compiler could
find. A multitude of ingenious and acute hypotheses followed one another, as to the principle on
which the documents were selected, the reasons for
the chronological confusion which reigns in the
latter part of the eighth book, the date and
possible authorship of the compilation. Might not
the work be a sort of political manifesto produced
in the interest of Gregory's cause against the
Empire? Was not the author perhaps Cardinal
Deusdedit, the eminent canonist? or was the book

---

making a total of 363. But a good many numbers include more
than one document. Besides double numbers, a letter is often
entered *a pari*; that is, several copies were made and sent to the
different persons named in it, with the necessary changes in the
address and, if required, in the date. It may be added that the
numbering of the letters is not contemporary.

[1] See Giesebrecht, de Registro Gregorii VII emendando
(1858); Jaffé, preface to Monum. Greg. (1865), and Reg. Pontif.
i. 594.

[2] One writer alone, unless I am mistaken, ventured to oppose
the prevailing opinion; and that was Father Lapôtre, who also
anticipated Dr Caspar in his conclusions as to the Register of
John VIII. But he did not elaborate his argument. See
L'Europe et la Saint-Siège à l'Époque Carolingienne, i., Le Pape
Jean VIII (1895), 18 ff.

not completed until the time of Urban II or even later[1]? These and many other questions have in the main been set at rest by the results of a twice repeated analysis of the manuscript itself.

This work has been done with extreme elaborateness by Father Wilhelm M. Peitz[2] and Dr Erich Caspar[3], who have established the fact that the book is not a selection at all, but the actual Register of Gregory VII, carried on from month to month under the Pope's supervision[4]. It is not a transcript from the original documents, nor from an existing Register; nor is it a select or special Register made concurrently with a larger general

---

[1] References to most of this extensive literature are given in the works cited in the two following notes, and need not be repeated here.

[2] Das Originalregister Gregors VII, in Sitzungsberichte der Kaiserlichen Akademie in Wien, Philosophisch-Historische Klasse, clxv. 5 (1911), 1–354. Father Peitz's main conclusion has been admitted by scholars whose opinion is of unquestioned weight: M. Tangl, in Neues Archiv, xxxvii. (1912), 363 ff. ; E. von Ottenthal, in Mittheilungen, xxxiii. (1912), 142 ff. I have therefore adopted it in my text. But I am bound to say that the Father's manner of treatment excites suspicion. He is too positive in his statements, and his cavalier attitude towards other scholars does not encourage confidence. His line of argument is over-refined, and he makes many assumptions which call for proof. But what perhaps more than all leads me to hold my judgment in suspense is the fact that Father Peitz bases his conclusions first and foremost on palaeographical grounds; the text and practically all the rubrics are in one and the same hand. Now the rubrics, it seems, have gone by the board (see below, p. 128, note 3). I am not at all sure that the argument about the text may not also have to be profoundly modified.

[3] Studien zum Register Gregors VII, in Neues Archiv, xxxviii. (1913), 143–226.

[4] Peitz, p. 92.

Register; it is the only one that was ever composed[1]. The entries were copied from the corrected
draughts of the documents. The volume is all
written, with the exception of two or three inserted
pieces, in one hand; and Father Peitz contended
that this hand was that of the notary Rainerius,
whose name is found in documents from 1067 to
1080[2], but this cannot be regarded as proved[3].
The importance of the general result is first that
it settles the authenticity of the contents of the
Register[4], and secondly that it fixes the chronology
of the letters. It is not indeed to be supposed that
each letter was necessarily entered at the exact
time when it was drawn up. If there was a press
of business or if the Pope's movements were
disturbed, the draughts might be laid aside for
future registering, and when they were registered
the order might be disarranged. It is possible
that in the occasional absence of the Chancellor
registering would be deferred. A batch of letters
might be accidentally overlooked and then incorporated at a subsequent time. Besides, when
the Register was being written, it was not a bound

---

[1] P. 89. This last statement is of course one which cannot be
proved; it is disputed by Dr Otto Blaul in the Archiv für Urkundenforschung, iv. (1912), 114.

[2] Peitz, pp. 92–97.

[3] Nor was Father Peitz successful in his argument that the
rubrics, marginalia, &c., are in the same handwriting (pp. 22, 33 ff.).
This has been shown by Dr Caspar (pp. 149 ff.) not only on
palaeographical grounds but also from a comparison with an early
transcript of the book in the library at Troyes. Cf. E. von
Ottenthal, in Mittheilungen, xxxiii. 143 note.

[4] I may refer specially to the narrative of Gregory's election
(I. 1) and the much-discussed Dictatus Papae in II. 55a.

book but a series of loose quires. There are not a few instances in which fresh leaves or quires have been inserted, and these insertions might not always be put in the right places; some might be mislaid[1]. Still, down to book viii. 23, that is down to the spring of 1081, the chronological order is substantially maintained. After that point it breaks down: the next document belongs to near the end of 1083. There are scattered documents from Gregory's ninth and eleventh years; there is no trace that any Register was ever compiled for his tenth. The book ends abruptly in the middle of a sentence at some date in the winter of 1083–1084.

But the small size of the Register has not yet been accounted for. Father Peitz explains it on the principle that only documents dealing with difficult questions were inserted[2]: if there were several documents relating to a particular business, that which carried the matter a stage further, and so far settled it, would be registered; the others would be left on one side. This solution depends on a doubtful interpretation of what Giraldus Cambrensis said about the Registers of more than a century later[3], and the value of Giraldus' unsupported testimony is not free from suspicion. But it is certain that the Register was not composed on this basis, because we possess letters of Gregory not included in it which contain more important

---

[1] Thus in book III., the text of which appears not to have been transcribed concurrently with the writing of the documents, there is a gap of some five months, from September 1075 to February 1076.

[2] Pp. 205 ff.   [3] See below, p. 135, note 2.

decisions and definitions than those dealing with
the same matters which are found in it[1]. The truth
appears to be that after the second book was completed, the Chancery clerk became slack in writing
the Register. Documents were produced as required, but their registration was neglected. It
may naturally be conjectured that this lax performance of the routine of official business was to
a great extent due to the inevitable disorganization
which arose in a time of trouble and stress. But
there were some documents of which it was
essential to keep a record: these were the Acts of
Synods, and it has been acutely observed that it
was often the meeting of a Synod which served as
a stimulus to the Chancery official to resume his
labours[2]. In an index added to the volume in the
fourteenth century it was not inappropriately
entitled Registrum Epistolarum et Conciliorum[3].

The Register did not include Privileges. Only
one is comprised in it, and this is a confirmation
of the primacy of the Archbishop of Lyons: it was
entered because it contained prescriptions relative
to the purity of the prelate's election which laid
down definitions of canonical order. But it was
not transcribed in full; the prohibitive clauses
and the sanction at the end were omitted, and a
reference added to the Privilege contained 'at the
beginning of this book[4].' That such a separate
Register existed is proved by the fact that one

---

[1] Caspar, p. 198.

[2] See *ibid.* pp. 206–212, 215.

[3] Jaffé, Reg. i. 596.

[4] 'Et reliqua usque in finem, sicut in privilegio constat, quod
est in capite huius libelli': Reg. vi. 34.

Privilege still remains attached to a flyleaf preceding the text of the book, and this too is entered imperfectly with a reference to other documents before it[1]. We cannot tell how large this collection of Privileges was, but it is clear that the principle of separating such documents from the Letters was observed in Gregory's time[2]. When the volume was bound it may be presumed that these queries were intended to be kept distinct; but they were somehow lost sight of and disappeared, and only by chance a single Privilege was found and was prefixed to the volume.

The Privileges then were copied out into a separate Register, not because they were less important than Letters but because they formed a distinct class of documents. They were not consulted for the same reasons as Letters, and when they had to be referred to it was probably more convenient to seek them in a volume or set of volumes by themselves. Letters on the other hand were of much greater interest from the point of view of the Papal Court. It was necessary to have their decisions on matters of procedure, of order, of canon law accessible for ready reference; and this object was attained by keeping them apart from the copies of the Privileges, which usually extended to a much greater length.

If this plan was found desirable in the time of Gregory VII, one would have expected its advantages to have been still more recognized in the twelfth century, when the bulk of the Pope's correspondence must have increased tenfold. It may

---

[1] Peitz, pp. 122 f.　　　　[2] Caspar, pp. 213 f.

perhaps have been continued under Innocent II, whose Register, no longer preserved, appears to have been comprehended in a single volume[1]. But it is certain that from the time when we possess what claim to rank as complete Registers, that is, from the accession of Innocent III in 1198 onwards, Letters and Privileges are entered side by side. There is no attempt at classification, except that a special set of letters of a political nature was separated by Innocent from the rest and recorded in a Registrum super negotio Imperii[2]. The general Register was comprised in nineteen books, of which something more than ten remain to us in the handwriting of Innocent III's time[3]. Whether

---

[1] See Caspar, p. 217.

[2] This special Register contains a large proportion of letters addressed to the Pope.

[3] These are books I., II., and two portions of III., and books V.–XII. Books XIII.–XVI. are preserved in a later transcript. Of the whole of III., IV., and XIX. and of thirteen letters in XVIII. there exists a table of contents, which has been printed by A. Theiner, Vetera Monumenta Slavorum Meridionalium Historiam illustrantia, i. (1863), 47–70. From this it appears that book III. 1–42 are really letters 170–215, and 43–57 are letters 260–275; the numbers in the table are five higher because five letters entered *a pari* are counted separately. No trace remains of book XVII. A description of the Registers is given by Delisle in the Bibliothèque de l'École des Chartes, xlvi. (1885), 84–93; cf. Denifle, Die päpstlichen Registerbände des dreizehnten Jahrhunderts, in Archiv für Literatur- und Kirchen-Geschichte des Mittelalters, ii. (1888), 72–75 and notes. See also the introduction to Specimina palaeographica Regestorum Romanorum Pontificum, by Denifle and G. Palmieri (1888), and A. Luchaire, Les Registres d'Innocent III (1904). The Register of the eighth and ninth years passed into England in the eighteenth century and was acquired by the fourth Earl of Ashburnham in 1848. His son, the fifth Earl, presented it to the Vatican Archives in 1884.

they are the actual Registers drawn up from day to day or fair copies made for reference is not quite certain. Delisle first raised a doubt on the point[1], and he was supported by Heinrich Denifle, a man of immense learning and exactness, who was for many years in charge of the Vatican Archives[2]. It is probable that the Registrum super negotio Imperii is the only volume which contains the actual original Register, and that all the rest are contemporary transcripts from such Registers[3]. There is sufficient evidence to show that they were not copied directly from the original documents, still less from their draughts. But the critical question involved is of subordinate importance, for, if they be fair copies, it is not disputed that these were officially transcribed in the Chancery from Registers already made[4]; they only take us a stage further from the original texts. It is not maintained that the copyist was more than a copyist.

If this conclusion is correct, the original Register from which the existing volumes of Innocent III were transcribed differed from that of Gregory VII in that it was composed not from the corrected draughts, the *notae* or *minutae*, but from the finished documents after they were completed

---

[1] Especially with regard to book II.: Mémoire sur les Actes d'Innocent III, in Bibliothèque de l'École des Chartes, 4th series, iv. (1858), 6.

[2] Archiv, *ubi supra*, pp. 59–64.

[3] Father Peitz in his thoroughgoing way claimed the whole series as original Registers (*ubi supra*, pp. 159–184), but he was only successful in convincing scholars with regard to the Registrum super negotio Imperii. See Tangl, in Neues Archiv, xxxvii. 364 f.

[4] Cardinal Pitra alone held that books I. and II. were a private compilation: Analecta novissima, i. 173 (1885).

for dispatch[1]. This of course presupposes a much greater regularity of system and organization in the Chancery than it had previously been possible to secure[2]. After Innocent III's time, though the evidence is conflicting[3], it seems on the whole probable that the same method was pursued with regard to Privileges and Litterae de Gratia, but that Letters produced at the initiative of the Curia were registered from the draughts. It may be that the distinction arose from the fact that the former classes of documents were not necessarily registered unless a fee was paid[4], and if a man had to pay a fee it is natural to suppose that he would demand that the registration should be made from the completed document. This question of fees also worked in another direction. The recipient who had already been put to expense in obtaining his Privilege or Letters would often be satisfied with the possession of his document, and would spare the further payment for registration[5]. But economy was not the only cause of the incomplete-

[1] Cf. Kaltenbrunner, Römische Studien, i., in Mittheilungen, v. (1884), 234 f.

[2] In all probability the earliest known Registers were transcribed from originals (above, pp. 31 f.). It is in the transitional period, represented by the Registers of John VIII and Gregory VII, that they were taken from draughts.

[3] For the extensive literation on this subject see the references in Bresslau, i. 116 and 117 notes.

[4] This is inferred from a notice of exemption from such payments in particular cases; 'pro regestro ab eisdem nichil dari consuevit': Tangl, Päpstliche Kanzleiordnungen, p. 66, n. 6, 1894. Cf. Kaltenbrunner, p. 240.

[5] Every English Cathedral muniment room which I have examined contains large numbers of Papal rescripts, in originals or copies, which are not to be found in the Registers.

ness of the Registers, because they do not contain all the Litterae de Curia[1], and for these of course no payment for registration was ever made. It was believed in the twelfth century that all documents relating to important matters were entered in the Registers[2]. But as a fact they are by no means complete even in regard to the political correspondence, a record of which, it might seem, it was essential to preserve in an official form. No satisfactory principle of selection has been suggested, and it is probable that the defective character of the Registers is due to the overwhelming mass of business which confronted the staff of the Chancery[3] and possibly also to the negligence of the officials whose duty it was to draw up the Registers[4].

[1] Innocent IV attempted to make provision for their regular record by the institution of a distinct Register of Litterae Curiales.

[2] Bishop Stephen of Tournay says, 'Consuetudo est Romanae ecclesiae quod, cum alicui de magno negotio mittit epistolam, apud se retinet eius exemplum': Summa, dist. LXXXI., p. 104, ed. J. F. von Schulte, 1891. No doubt Giraldus Cambrensis meant the same thing when he wrote, 'Registrum autem suum facit papa quilibet, hoc est librum ubi transcripta privilegiorum omnium et literarum sui temporis super magis arduis causis continentur': De Invectionibus, IV. 9 (Opera, iii., ed. J. S. Brewer, 1863, p. 90). Father Peitz thought that he referred to more difficult matters: see above, p. 129.

[3] As it stands, the Register of Innocent III is enormously more copious than that of Gregory VII. The parts preserved contain 3702 letters (Delisle, p. 10), and there exist the headings of 720 more (see above, p. 132, note 3). If we assume the lost XVIIth book and the XVIIIth, of which only scanty traces remain, to have included some 400 letters—a moderate estimate—we arrive at a total of about 4800.

[4] On the whole question of the reasons which determined the inclusion of documents in the Register see R. von Heckel, in

Having now considered the types of documents produced in the Papal Chancery and examined the manner in which they were recorded down to the thirteenth century, I propose to go back and briefly summarize the main lines on which the Chancery developed from the earliest times down to the point at which I interrupted its history at the pontificate of Calixtus II, and then to pursue that history for a century longer, with a glance onwards to later times.

We have seen how the Pope's secretarial office originated in the college of notaries attached to the regions of the city. Of its seven principal officers six might be charged with the duty of 'dating' documents, while the lowest only, the Protoscriniarius, was responsible for writing them. The office in which they were written was the Scrinium, and the handwriting employed was the old Roman cursive, or Curial, hand. In the eighth century, under Carolingian influences, the two successive acts of writing and dating became marked by distinct entries in the documents; and almost at the same moment we find for the first time that the person who dates documents was not any member of the notarial college but the Pope's Librarian, who also adopts (though not certainly until the eleventh century) the Frankish title of Chancellor[1]. In the eleventh century also the beautiful Carolingian Minuscule began to invade the Chancery. During all the fluctuations of

Archiv für Urkundenforschung, i. 430–442, and for later Registers, pp. 488–500.

[1] Above, pp. *12–19, 51–57.*

usage during that time of change—of reform and reaction—we find the general rule to prevail, that documents written at Rome were produced by the old notaries or Scriniarii in their traditional Curial hand but were dated by the Pope's personal officer, the Librarian, who wrote in Minuscule[1].

When however from the time of Leo IX the Pope, as often happened, was more frequently absent from Rome than resident at the Lateran, he had to make such arrangements as he found possible, and to employ local scribes at the various places where he might be. Thus the handwriting changes according to the circumstances, but the rule of the dating by the Chancellor and Librarian remains established. One result of this change of conditions was that outside Rome these occasional scribes omitted to record their names: the Scriptum more and more disappeared from the documents. Through Imperial influences also it came about that the Archbishop of Cologne, who was Arch-Chancellor of Italy, should be regarded as head also of the Papal Chancery. He was such no doubt in 1023 and again about 1051; but the practice was intermittent. At certain times the bishop of Selva Candida seemed established in this position[2]. The very titles employed by the officials indicate the manner in which the Pope was attempting to establish a personal staff of clerks to take the place of the notaries whom he found on the spot: they came to describe themselves as notaries not of the Holy Apostolic Church but of the Sacred Lateran Palace, and as they were

---

[1] Above, pp. 64 f.   [2] Pp. 60 ff.

in no way necessarily connected with the traditional Roman system, or indeed with Rome itself, it was natural that they should more and more use the Minuscule handwriting which was current among educated people in the west rather than the unpleasing and difficult Cursive which was the mark of the Scrinium. After Calixtus II the local Scriniarii ceased to be employed[1], and with their cessation the Scriptum was discontinued.

This double change, the omission of the Scriptum and with it the final abandonment of the Curial hand, made a conspicuous difference in the general aspect of the documents, but for the next twenty years no change occurred in the uniformity of the Chancery organization[2]. The regular datary continued to be described as Chancellor or Librarian, or both[3]; but from the death of Celestine II in 1144 he ceased to be Librarian[4]. The Archives and the Library were now separated, and each had its own chief officer[5]. The Chancellor is now regularly a Cardinal Priest or Cardinal Deacon, never a Cardinal Bishop, except once under the Antipope Calixtus III (1168–1178) when the Cardinal Bishop of Tusculum makes his appearance[6]. The Chancellor almost always held his post for life or until he became Pope, as Gelasius II, Lucius II, Alexander III, and Gregory VIII. The only

---

[1] The name appears for some time longer, but only to indicate Notaries Public, who were appointed by the Pope but not for any service in the Chancery: see Bresslau, i. 267.

[2] For the following see Bresslau, i. 240–248, where lists of the officers are given.   [3] Spec. 57 (2), 59.

[4] Nouveau Traité de Diplomatique, v. 266.

[5] Bresslau, i. 240, note 3.   [6] Spec. 94 (3), 95.

example of a change being made took place at the accession of Innocent III, when Cencius the Chamberlain, who held the office, without bearing the title, of Chancellor, was superseded[1].

During this period the Chancellor invariably wrote his own name in the Datum; but after Calixtus II he ceased to write the whole date, and inserted his name or its initial in a space left vacant for the purpose[2]. But the fact that an autograph was required led necessarily to the frequent employment of deputies. For the Chancellor might be away on a mission[3] or engaged in other business, or he might be ill. His place was then filled in one of two ways. If he was absent from the Court for a long time, a Cardinal signed in his stead as Vice-Chancellor, *vices cancellarii gerens*[4]; but if his absence was only occasional, a deputy signed by his own rank or office, Subdiaconus et notarius, Capellanus et Scriptor, or the like, but did not describe himself as Vice-Chancellor[5]. This was the practice at least until 1187, and the latter rule was always adopted when the Chancellorship was actually vacant, as happened for four years under Eugenius III and for nearly twenty under Alexander III. It is possible that motives of economy had something to do with this; for the Vice-Chancellor received the fees due to the Chancellor, whereas if his duties were performed by another officer the fees were paid into the Pope's chest.

---

[1] See Bresslau, i. 243, cf. 242, note 6.　　[2] Spec. 64, 74, 80.

[3] Thus Chancellor Roland was sent as legate to Frederick I's court in October 1157: Rahewin, Gesta Friderici Imperatoris, iii. 9.

[4] Spec. 81 (1).　　　　　　　　[5] Spec. 74 at foot.

The Antipope Calixtus III employed persons of
a lower dignity than Cardinals as Vice-Chancellors;
and his example was followed by Urban III, who
made Moyses, a Canon of the Lateran, Vice-
Chancellor in 1187.   The Chancellorship was then
left vacant by Gregory VIII and Clement III, and
Moyses, contrary to the earlier practice, continued
in office[1].   When however in 1191 Celestine III
once more appointed a Chancellor, Moyses reverted
to his proper rank and signed documents as Subdeacon and Canon.   But the precedent established
by his former position was not without influence.
Innocent III began by not reappointing the acting
Chancellor Cencius, and he allowed three notaries
in succession to sign as Vice-Chancellors.   At last
in 1205 he appointed a Chancellor and the title of
Vice-Chancellor disappeared for twelve years.   In
1213 this Chancellor died and a vacancy followed,
in which a Notary and Subdeacon executed the
duties of the office.   It is possible that he was
made Chancellor in the last year of Innocent's
pontificate; but if so, he was the last of the line.
From the accession of the next Pope, Honorius III,
no Chancellor was ever appointed.

The importance of the change consisted in the
fact that thenceforward the Vice-Chancellor, who
now became the real head of the Chancery, was
regularly appointed from outside the ranks of the
Cardinals.   He was now chosen not for his dignity
but for his special competence; he rose from the
lower offices of the Chancery to be the head of his
department, and he almost invariably held the

[1] Spec. 99, 98.

degree of *magister*. In one single instance in the course of the thirteenth century a Vice-Chancellor was made a Cardinal and retained his office, but he was not a Cardinal when he became Vice-Chancellor. He dates documents at first as *cancellarii vicem agens*, but towards the middle of the century the substantive *vicecancellarius* begins to be used[1]. The Vice-Chancellor was inevitably becoming a more and more important person, and it was natural that he should be admitted to the college of Cardinals, as the Chancellor had been in the twelfth century. Hence from the time of Boniface VIII it became usual to create him a Cardinal soon after his appointment. In fact from 1296 the practice became invariable, with the single exception of Peter, elect of Palentia, who held office only from November 1306 to his death in September 1307[2]. But so soon as it had become customary that a Vice-Chancellor should be made a Cardinal, it was an easy step to allow that *vice versa* a Cardinal might be made Vice-Chancellor. This seems to have become the rule under John XXII, and so the reform effected by Honorius III in the interests of administrative efficiency was abandoned[3]. In the time of Clement VII, in 1532, the office of Vice-Chancellor was permanently attached to the Cardinal of the title

---

[1] See Bresslau, i. 249, note 2. On the rare occasions when there was a vacancy in the office the acting deputy signs by his rank, as *capellanus et notarius* (1222–1226), *subdiaconus et notarius* (1256–1257).

[2] Bresslau, i. 255 f.

[3] From the fourteenth century the place of the Vice-Chancellor was often taken by a deputy, *regens cancellariam: ibid.* i. 289 ff.

of S. Lorenzo in Damaso[1]. But long before this he had ceased to take any active share in the productions of the Chancery. It is said that the last appearance of his name in the Datum of a Bull is under Clement VI (1342–1352)[2]. The practical charge of the business of the Chancery passed into other hands.

[1] A. Cocquelines, Bullarum Romanorum Pontificum Collectio amplissima, iv. (1745), 99.

[2] Nouveau Traité de Diplomatique, v. 305.

VII.

In the twelfth century, as causes were evoked to Rome in constantly increasing numbers, the Papal Court developed a high degree of efficiency in defining questions of law. These lie outside our province; but in the course of the preliminary enquiries it was necessary to inspect and verify documents. On such occasions the assistance of the officials of the Chancery could probably as a rule be dispensed with, for the College of Cardinals usually included some members who had experience of its technical business. It is of interest to notice how in these circumstances principles of criticism were by degrees evolved, and I shall give some examples of English cases to illustrate the manner in which this criticism was performed. The narratives come from writers who were naturally partisans; but I am concerned not with the merits of the particular cases, but with the points to which, in dealing with the genuineness of documents, the Papal Court attached importance.

I take my first example from the proceedings which arose in connexion with the notorious claim of the Archbishop of Canterbury to primacy over York. This claim was based on a series of nine documents which were forged under the direction of Archbishop Lanfranc in 1072, and was accepted on their authority by the English Court[1]. But though Archbishops of York might be constrained to make their profession personally to the Archbishop of Canterbury, they never admitted his right to demand it. The documents were sent to Rome but were left unnoticed. In 1102, if we may believe a letter written by the Chapter of York, enquiry was made of the Chancellor, John of Gaetà, as to what evidence there was at Rome bearing on the dispute between the two Churches, and he replied that Rome knew nothing except what was contained in the Register of Gregory the Great[2]; and Gregory, we know, had granted no primacy to Canterbury, he granted it to either Archbishop according to seniority of consecration. It is significant that in the long and elaborate statement of the case for Canterbury which Archbishop Ralph addressed to Calixtus II in 1120, he made no allusion to the forged documents[3].

At length in 1123 when both the Archbishops, William of Canterbury and Thurstan of York, were in Rome, the representatives of Canterbury took the opportunity of discussing the question, though not as actual litigants, before the Papal

---

[1] See H. Boehmer, Die Fälschungen Erzbischof Lanfranks von Canterbury, 1902.

[2] 'Denique decanus [Eboracensis], quando fuit Romae cum Girardo archiepiscopo, sicut ipse testatur, a cancellario Romanae ecclesiae diligenter perscrutatus est de contentione harum ecclesiarum, quid inde Roma sentiret et quid in decretis suis haberet; at ille dixit Roma[m] nec aliud sentire nec habere quam quod in registro beati Gregorii scriptum est': Historians of the Church of York, ed. J. Raine, ii. (1886), 113 f.

[3] The letter is printed *ibid.*, pp. 228–250. For the date see Boehmer, p. 41 note.

Court. The narrative which we possess comes
from York; and although there is no doubt that
in the matter at issue York was right and Canterbury was wrong, we must remember in reading
the account of Hugh the Chantor that he writes
throughout as the defender of the claims of his
Church. The Canterbury documents, he tells us[1],
were ordered to be read.

They were indeed entitled with the names of Roman
pontiffs, but they did not at all savour of the Roman style.
When they had been read, and then at last that of St Gregory
to Augustine concerning the distinction of the two metro-
politans of England, some of the Romans asked them of
Canterbury whether those Privileges had seals (*bullas*); and
they said that they had left the sealed documents in the
Church and had brought transcripts of them. And because it
is not necessary to give faith to unsealed or unauthenticated[2]
Privileges or charters, they were asked whether they would
swear that they had originals of them with seals. They
withdrew, and consulting among themselves they said that
the documents bore no seals. But one wished to persuade
the others that he should swear for the cause of his Church,
which was no doubt sound and lawful advice. The others
however refused, fearing to perjure themselves if they swore
that the documents were sealed. They decided to return and
say that the seals were perished or lost. But when they made
this statement, some smiled, others wrinkled their noses,
others broke forth into laughter and said that it was very
odd that the lead was perished or lost and that the parchment
was preserved. Some may perchance think that this story
is made up and the narrator is talking nonsense; but it is as
true as it seems fictitious. Afterwards they said that possibly
at that time seals were not in use. But the Romans bore
testimony that there were seals from the time of St Gregory

---

[1] Historians of the Church of York, ii. 204 ff.
[2] 'Non bullatis vel non signatis.'

and that some sealed Privileges of his were still preserved in the Roman Church. So, as they had nothing more to say on the matter, they departed in confusion, and their Privileges were neither received with trust nor their words with praise or favour.

The Pope then called upon the Archbishop of York to produce his evidences. Thurstan replied that he had brought none with him, because he had come to attend a Council, not as a party to a lawsuit. On being pressed however he admitted that his companions had chanced, without having been asked, to bring with them some letters unsealed as well as a copy of their Privilege. The Court desired them to be produced and read. The documents consisted of the Letter of St Gregory to Augustine which had already been brought forward by the representatives of Canterbury, and that of Honorius I to the two Archbishops, together with four recent Letters of Urban II and his three successors. An examination was made of the letters and no questions were asked about the seals, for the documents were well known: *omnes enim bene noverant.* Possibly the modern documents were verified in the Registers, the early ones in Bede or in some compilation of Papal letters. The discussion of course led to no result, because there were no parties empowered to promote an appeal, and there was no question before the Court with which it could deal judicially.

From this account it is clear that the first thing to which the Papal Court attached import- ance was the authentication of documents produced by their leaden seals. In the absence of the seals recourse was had to materials in the Papal archives. The narrator says that the documents produced by his adversaries were not written in the Roman style, but he does not tell us that this point was considered by the Court. On one matter, according to his statement, they displayed ignorance, for they assumed that the original documents should have been written on parchment, whereas if genuine they would undoubtedly have been on papyrus.

In the same way, eighty years later, when the Bishop of Worcester appealed to Rome on the question of the exemption of the monastery of Evesham, the only criticism made on the actual documents produced related to the genuineness of their seals. The case came before Innocent III towards the end of 1205, and it was argued at length. Thomas of Marlborough, a monk of Evesham, who was proctor for the monastery and wrote a narrative of the whole affair[1], made a full statement of the rights which it claimed, and alleged two Bulls of Pope Constantine, of the years 709 and 710, as well as recent Indults of Clement III and Celestine III[2]. The documents of Constantine were rank forgeries of the tenth century[3]. Upon this Master Robert of Clipstone, who appeared for the Bishop, replied

[1] Chronicon Abbatiae de Evesham, pp. 141–200, ed. W. D. Macray, 1863.   [2] Pp. 154–158.

[3] They are printed *ibid.*, pp. 171–173. Dr M. Spaethen, who has published an interesting paper on the Evesham case in Neues Archiv, xxxi. (1906), 629–649, supposes the forgeries to have been made in the twelfth century. But they were known by

Holy Father, our adversary would have well said, if the Privileges, in which he finds all the force and power of his contentions and which he lays as the foundation of his whole case, were genuine; whereas they are false, [though, he implies, we cannot prove it]. For the parchment (*carta*) and style, the string and the seal of the Privileges of Constantine are entirely unknown in our country. But the bearer of the Indults of Clement and Celestine was Nicholas of Warwick, a notorious forger, and therefore we believe them to be spurious; and we say the same of the others.

And the Lord Pope [proceeds Marlborough] commanded that I should exhibit them, and I did so. And the Lord Pope felt them with his own hands, and pulled them by the seal and parchment, if perchance he could separate the seal from the string. After examining them very carefully he passed them to the Cardinals for examination; and when they had gone round the circle and come back to the Pope, he held up the Privilege of Constantine and said, 'Privileges of this sort, which to you are unknown, are to us very well known, and they could not be forged.' And holding up the Indults he said, 'These are genuine'; and he handed them all back to me[1].

Marlborough himself had no part in the fraud; he merely produced documents which he was ordered to produce, and he confesses that he had no knowledge whatever about the characteristics of Constantine's documents. On this matter probably Innocent was no better informed. He was not, it seems, then aware that parchment was not

the beginning of the eleventh: see Haddan and Stubbs, Councils and Ecclesiastical Documents, iii. (1871), 279 note. The Papal subscription which Dr Spaethen assigns to the twelfth century (pp. 642 f.) is a feature of the Anglo-Saxon type of document. But the Bulls were probably touched up after the time of Lanfranc, as the qualification of the Archbishop of Canterbury as 'Brittanniarum primas' suggests (cf. Boehmer, *ubi supra*, p. 83); but the use of this title is not decisive (see *ibid.*, p. 91 notes 3 and 4).

[1] Chronicon Abbatiae de Evesham, pp. 160 f.

used in the time of Constantine[1]; very likely he had never seen one of his seals: the only test he applied was directed to ascertain whether the seal and the document belonged to one another; in other words, whether a forged document had been attached to a genuine seal. In any case, he was grossly deceived, and in the elaborate confirmation of the exemption of the monastery which he caused to be drawn up he recited both the alleged Privileges of Constantine[2]. The truth was that, however well acquainted he might be with regard to the current practice of the Chancery and the forms of documents in use for a long time earlier, he was entirely without the means of judging the genuineness of a document professing to be five hundred years old. There were no materials for its criticism.

As yet we have found that the one practical test applied to the examination of the genuineness of a Bull consisted in the inspection of the seal and of its attachment to the document. The same method, according to Giraldus Cambrensis, appears to have been used when in 1199–1200 he brought before the Papal Court his appeal against the failure of his election to the bishopric of

---

[1] He had occasion later to learn that papyrus was the material employed: see below, pp. 160 f.

[2] 18 January 1205, Reg. viii. 204. While the Pope's critical faculty was at fault, his legal acuteness prevented him from allowing the monastery the jurisdiction over the Deanery of the Vale. Hence, when his rescript was inserted in an abbreviated form (mentioning only one Privilege of Constantine) in the Decretals of Gregory IX, v. xxxiii. 17, it became a leading authority for the doctrine that the exemption of a religious house did not involve the exemption of its 'members.'

St David's; but his statement suggests a further stage of criticism. Two letters, he says, of Lucius II and Eugenius III were produced by him: they were inspected and read, and the seals were observed[1]. The letters were read in order that the Court might be apprised of their legal content; they were inspected in order that it might be ascertained whether there was anything about the parchment, the manner of writing, and perhaps the formulae, to excite suspicion. That Innocent III was alive to the importance of examining the literary structure of a text is shown from a question which, Giraldus tells us, arose in connexion with a document of a different sort.

He was interested not only in securing his own election to the see of St David's, but also in asserting that Church's independence of the Archbishop of Canterbury. Now, one evening he was discussing the matter with the Pope in his chamber, when Innocent ordered the Register to be brought 'in which were enumerated for the whole Christian world both the metropolitical churches of each kingdom in order and the episcopal churches suffragan to them.' The part relating to England was read: 'The metropolis of Canterbury has these suffragan churches, Rochester, London,' and the rest in order. After this there was a rubric *Of Wales*, and the text continued: 'In Wales the church of St David's, Llandaff, Bangor, and St Asaph.' The Pope smiled and said, 'You see,

[1] 'Quibus inspectis et lectis et auditis, et bullis notatis': De Iure Menevensis Ecclesiae, III., Opera, iii. (ed. Brewer, 1863), 188.

St David's is numbered among them.' Giraldus replied, 'But it and the other churches of Wales are not numbered in the same way as the suffragans of England, that is, in the accusative. If they were, they might certainly be reckoned subject.' 'That is a good point,' said the Pope; 'and there is another thing which makes for you and your church. There is a rubric inserted, which is nowhere done in the Register, except where it passes from kingdom to kingdom or from province to province.' 'True,' quickly rejoined Giraldus, 'and Wales is a part of the English kingdom, and not a kingdom by itself.' The Pope did not commit himself further than to remark cautiously, 'You may take it that our Register is not against you.' The facts here stated can be verified. We possess a Provinciale of the type described in the Gesta of Cardinal Albinus written in 1188 or 1189, which presents the grammatical features and the rubrication mentioned by Giraldus; but it is probable that the actual volume to which reference was made was an earlier Register of the time of Alexander III[1].

Forgery has always been a favourite occupation, and it has prevailed at all times when the literary skill required for its exercise was available. In the middle ages it was employed especially with the object of acquiring rights of property or jurisdiction or of obtaining benefices or other desirable grants. As a large proportion of such documents related to ecclesiastical lands and offices, very

---

[1] See below, Appendix VI.

many claims needed the support of the Pope's authority; and it became essential, for the protection of persons whose rights or interests were affected, that the correct forms of his documents should be understood.   Hence the books of Formularies which were drawn up for the use of notaries contained many rules and specimens of the types which genuine Papal Letters ought to present[1]. But these models, which were set out as guides against deception, served in their turn as materials for the unscrupulous, and simplified the work of forgery.   It was urgently necessary to take steps to check the evil, and Innocent III determined to deal vigorously with it.   All through his pontificate he was ceaselessly on the watch for the detection of forged documents.   In May of his first year he found that letters had been produced bearing seals of Celestine III and himself which were not genuine. He issued a Decretal on the matter, in which he first laid down general rules to safeguard the procedure by which Bulls were obtained.   He forbade that anyone should receive Letters at Rome except from the Pope's own hands or from his duly appointed official[2]; only persons of great authority were permitted to employ a messenger[3].

---

[1] There are a good many examples of the thirteenth century printed in Rockinger's Briefsteller und Formelbücher.

[2] This was the Bullator, as appears from Reg. I. 349 (below p. 156, note 1).

[3] 'Accidit enim nuper in Urbe quod quidam huiusmodi falsitatis astutiam perniciosius exercentes, in suis fuere iniquitatibus deprehensi; ita quod bullas tam sub nomine nostro quam bonae memoriae Celestini PP. praedecessoris nostri, quas falso

Innocent then passed to the particular case brought before him. He commanded the Archbishop of Rheims—and a letter in the same terms was addressed to all archbishops and their suffragans severally—to make enquiry into the reception of suspicious Letters. The first test to be employed was the comparison of the forged seal with a genuine one[1]; and to assist the examination the Pope caused one of the spurious seals to be appended to the document together with the authentic *bulla*. A few months later a case arose in which a clerk of Milan had made use of a Mandate requiring the Chapter to admit him to a canonry and prebend. The Chapter referred back the document for the Pope's consideration, and he at once had doubts about its genuineness. The style of composition and the manner of writing were indeed a little suspicious, but the seal was genuine. Careful examination however showed that the seal was a little swollen on the upper part, and the Pope was able without difficulty to draw out the string, while the other end of the string protruding from the lower part of the seal remained unmoved. The inference

confixerunt, et quamplures litteras bullis signatas eisdem invenimus apud eos, ipsosque captos adhuc in carcere detinemus. Nos autem...districtius inhibemus ne quis apud sedem apostolicam de caetero litteras nostras nisi a nobis vel de manibus illorum recipiat qui de mandato nostro sunt ad illud officium deputati. Si vero persona tantae auctoritatis exstiterit ut deceat eum per nuntium litteras nostras recipere, nuntium ipsum ad cancellariam nostram vel ad nos ipsos mittat idoneum, per quem litteras apostolicas iuxta formam praescriptam recipiat': Reg. I. 235, 19 May 1198; cf. Decret. Greg. IX, v. xx. 4.

[1] 'Primo fiat collatio de falsa bulla cum vera': Reg., l.c.

was clear: a genuine seal had been detached from
the document to which it belonged by cutting the
string;· the seal had then been heated at the upper
part in order to admit of the insertion of a new
string joining it to the forged letter, but the other
end of the old string was left hanging from the
lower part[1].

The Pope proceeded to draw up a fuller and
more elaborate set of rules for the criticism of
disputed documents. He enumerates five marks
of forgery. First, the seal itself might be spurious.
We have just seen that in another case Innocent
prescribed the comparison of suspicious seals with
ones acknowledged to be genuine. If no undoubted specimen was at hand, it is probable that
the practice then was, as it certainly was not
much later, to count the number of points or dots
in the circumference and on other parts of the
seal, in order to see whether they agreed with

---

[1] Caeterum cum easdem litteras, sicut viri providi et discreti,
ad nostram remisissetis praesentiam, ut ex earum inspectione
plenius nosceremus utrum ex nostra conscientia processissent, plus
in eis invenimus quam vestra fuisset discretio suspicata. Nam licet
in stylo dictaminis et forma scripturae aliquantulum coeperimus
dubitare, bullam tamen veram invenimus; quod primum nos
in vehementem admirationem induxit, cum litteras ipsas sciremus
de nostra conscientia nullatenus emanasse. Bullam igitur hinc
inde diligentius intuentes, in superiori parte, qua filo adhaeret,
eam aliquantulum tumentem invenimus; et cum filum ex parte
tumenti sine violentia qualibet aliquantulum attrahi fecissemus,
bulla in filo altero remanente, filum ex parte illa ab ipsa sine
qualibet difficultate avulsum, in cuius summitate adhuc etiam
incisionis indicium apparebat, per quod liquido deprehendimus
bullam illam ex aliis litteris extractam fuisse ac illis per vitium
falsitatis insertam, sicut ex litteris ipsis plenius agnoscetis, quas
ad maiorem certitudinem vobis duximus remittendas: Reg. i.
349, 4 September 1198.

what was known to be the correct number[1]. Secondly, the seal might be genuine but the original string completely removed and a new one inserted to attach it to a forged document. Thirdly, the string might be cut under the fold of the parchment, where it would not at once be noticed, and the seal attached to a forged letter, the string being mended with another string of similar texture; or again, fourthly, the string might be cut at the upper part of the seal, then passed through a spurious document and reinserted into the lead. This latter plan was that adopted in the case which provoked the issue of Innocent's Decretal: the test would be the condition of the lead, whether it showed signs of having been heated. Fifthly, genuine letters might be falsified by a slight erasure[2].

The Pope then mentions two grounds for suspicion which are more difficult to detect: if a

---

[1] Once an appellant alleged a letter to be spurious for lack of one point, 'litteras arguens falsitatis, et bullam volens astruere, quia punctus deerat, esse falsam': Reg. XIII. 54. In a paper on Léopold Delisle, published in the Proceedings of the British Academy, 1911–1912, p. 216, I stated erroneously that the Pope condemned the document. This was not so. The Mandate called in question was a Commission to enquire into the facts. It did not come up for scrutiny at Rome, because the Pope evoked the parties to appear before him and re-heard the case himself. For the points on the seal see Appendix VII. 4.

[2] Two further rules are added in the Decretals of Gregory IX. Sixthly, parts of a letter might be effaced by some chemical and the parchment blanched with chalk or some other application, and new writing inserted; or again, seventhly, the whole text might be deleted and a thin sheet of parchment glued on to the surface, and then a fresh document written on it. These are not found in Innocent's Register, or in Rainerius' Prima Collectio Decretalium Innocentii III, i. 14 (Migne, ccxvi. 1219).

document is obtained in an unauthorized way; or if a forged letter is cleverly presented for sealing among a budget of documents, and it is inadvertently accepted and sealed. In such cases it is necessary to examine the document in its literary composition, in its form of writing, and in the quality of the parchment. This last criterion would only be appreciated by the experts of the Chancery; the other two have already been considered. They depend on the rules of Dictamen, the observance of the Cursus; and on the laws for drawing up particular kinds of documents. Finally, attention is again directed to the manner in which the strings are attached and to the collation of the seal with an undoubted specimen: careful inspection will discover falsity if the die has moved or if the impression is blunt, if the seal is not level but rises in one part and is depressed in another[1].

---

[1] Prima species falsitatis haec est, ut falsa bulla litteris apponatur. Secunda, ut filum de vera bulla extrahatur ex toto, et per aliud filum immissum falsis litteris inseratur. Tertia, ut filum ab ea parte, in qua charta plicatur, incisum, cum vera bulla falsis litteris immittatur sub eadem plicatura cum filo similis canapis restauratum. Quarta, quod a superiori parte bullae altera pars fili sub plumbo rescinditur et per id[em] filum litteris falsis inserta reducitur infra plumbum. Quinta, cum litteris bullatis et redditis aliquid in eis per rasuram tenuem immutatur. [Sexta, cum scriptura litterarum, quibus fuerat apposita vera bulla, cum aqua vel vino universaliter abolita seu deleta, eadem charta cum calce et aliis iuxta consuetum artificium dealbata de novo rescribitur. Septima cum chartae cui fuerat apposita vera bulla, totaliter abolitae vel abrasae, alia subtilissima charta eiusdem quantitatis scripta cum tenacissimo glutino coniungitur.] Eos etiam a crimine falsitatis non reputamus immunes qui contra constitutionem praemissam scienter litteras nostras nisi de nostra vel bullatoris nostri manu recipiunt. Eos quoque qui accidentes ad bullas [*leg.* bullam] falsas litteras

With what precise care Innocent pursued his enquiries *in modo dictaminis* and *in forma scripturae* may be briefly illustrated. The style of address was particularly technical. A bishop is *venerabilis frater*; any one else, even an elected bishop before consecration, is *dilectus filius*[1]. But a special distinction, as we know from Formularies, was reserved for Emperors and Kings: such a

caute proiiciunt, ut de vera bulla cum aliis sigillentur. Sed hae duae species falsitatis non possunt facile deprehendi, nisi vel in modo dictaminis vel in forma scripturae vel qualitate chartae falsitas cognoscatur. In caeteris autem diligens indagator falsitatem poterit diligentius intueri vel in adiunctione filorum vel in collatione bullae vel motione vel obtusione; praesertim si bulla non sit aequalis sed alicubi magis sit tumida, alibi magis depressa: Reg. I. 349. The sentences in brackets are added from the text of the Decretals of Gregory IX, v. xx. 5.

[1] See the letter to the Archbishop of Antivari, 5 December 1200, in which Innocent states the grounds for condemning a Letter on which the Archbishop had acted: 'Nos vero rescriptum litterarum falsarum diligentius intuentes, in eis, tam in continentia quam in dictamine, manifeste deprehendimus falsitatem ac in hoc fuimus non modicum admirati quod tu tales litteras a nobis credideras emanasse, cum praesertim scire debeas sedem apostolicam in suis litteris consuetudinem hanc tenere, ut universos patriarchas, archiepiscopos, et episcopos *fratres*, caeteros autem, sive reges sint sive principes, vel alios homines cuiuscunque ordinis *filios*, in nostris litteris appellemus; et cum uni tantum personae litterae apostolicae dirigantur, nunquam ei loquamur in plurali, ut *vos* sive *vester* vel his similia in ipsis litteris apponantur. In falsis autem tibi litteris praesentatis, in salutatione *dilectus in Christo filius* vocabaris, cum in omnibus litteris quas aliquando tibi transmisimus te videre potueris a nobis *fratrem venerabilem* appellatum: propter quod sic esse te volumus in consimilibus circumspectum ut per falsas litteras denuo nequeas circumveniri vel falli, sed sic litteras apostolicas diligentius intueri tam in bulla quam in filo, tam etiam in carta quam stylo, quod veras pro falsis et falsas pro veris aliquomodo non admittas': Reg. III. 37. The document is included, with the blundered address 'Attinacensi episcopo,' in Gregory IX's Decretals, v. xx. 6.

person is not *dilectus filius* but *charissimus in Christo filius,* and after his name is added *imperator* or *rex illustris*; and in the Text of the letter *filius* must be followed by *noster*[1]. The name of a bishopric or monastery must be written in a Latin form ; if it appears in the vernacular the Letter is spurious[2]. The Pope now always

[1] The *noster* was here essential, but its use was not strictly confined to royal personages. The solecism of introducing it into the Address is not mentioned in the rules De Salutatione apostolica, printed by Delisle, Mémoire, pp. 68 ff., which are assigned to the end of the twelfth century; nor is it found in a Formulary of a century later, cited (*ibid.,* p. 29 note 1) from the Paris MS. 4163, where it is laid down, 'Vocat eos *carissimos in Christo filios*...in salutatione. In prosecutione vero litterarum addit *nostros.*' I doubt whether *nostro* appears in the Address in originals of the time of Innocent III. It is absent, for instance, from that Pope's Letter to John of England, 16 April 1214, printed *ex originali* in Rymer's Foedera, i. 119 (ed. 1816); cf. pp. 104, 117, 119. A letter of 14 May 1214 printed in Dachery's Spicilegium (ed. L. F. J. De la Barre, 1723), iii. 577, contains *nostro,* but the source of this document is not stated. By far the majority of Innocent's letters are preserved only with an abbreviated Address. Honorius III inserted *nostro* occasionally, to the King of Jerusalem (Epp. I. 1, ed. 1879), to Henry III (I. 162), and to Philip Augustus (I. 305, the letter is addressed to his son); but not, for instance, to the Emperor of Constantinople (I. 3) or to the Kings of Bohemia and Hungary (I. 157, 181).

[2] 'Praefatae litterae nequaquam de nostra conscientia manaverunt, quia cum monasterium ipsum, non solum publico sui nomine, verum etiam per sui negotia multiplicia, quae nos frequenter in instantia nostrae sollicitudinis occuparunt, notissimum nobis existat, verisimile non apparet quod eius monachi *de Burguol,* sicut in eisdem litteris continetur, Gallico idiomate scripsissemus, quos sermone Latino *Burgulienses* consuevimus appellare. In quo procul dubio deprehenditur quod si litterae ipse quomodocumque a nostro auditorio processerunt, fraudulenter fuit, ut insuetum, Gallicum nomen positum, ne per Latinum, ut assuetum, monasterium ipsum fuisset redditum nobis notum': Reg. XI. 144, 20 September 1208.

addressed an individual person in the singular, *tu* not *vos*[1]. This practice was established in the course of the twelfth century[2], and perhaps the use of the plural lingered longest in letters addressed to the Emperor[3].

But when documents alleged to be forgeries were produced before him Innocent refused to condemn them on grounds which he regarded as immaterial. On one occasion a document was denounced because, besides some irregularities of procedure, the capital *S* in *Salutem* was extended too far in the hinder stroke[4], and because it named an archdeacon before a dean; the Pope overruled the objections as frivolous and vain. Again, when a mandate was claimed as a forgery, the Pope on inspection found only an erasure of a few letters, and at once declared the document to

[1] See above, p. 22, note 2.

[2] The statement in the Nouveau Traité de Diplomatique, v. 174, that the last examples of the use of the plural in addressing an individual person are found in two letters of Alexander III to Suger Abbot of St Denis is not supported by the numerous specimens printed in the Recueil des Historiens de la France, xvi. 436–462.

[3] See Wolfgang Michael, Die Formen des unmittelbaren Verkehrs zwischen den Deutschen Kaisern und souveränen Fürsten (1888), pp. 78–97. The singular became uniform under Eugenius III. Conversely, about the same time Conrad III adopted the more distant plural in addressing the Pope. Frederick I in 1159, in a moment of irritation, restored the singular, and a lively passage of arms ensued. See *ibid.*, pp. 98–119, and Rahewin's narrative, Gesta Friderici Imperatoris, iv. 19–22. The matter was complicated by the fact that Frederick insisted on placing his name before the Pope's in the Address.

[4] 'Quia *S* littera capitalis in hac dictione *Salutem* nimis erat in longum a posteriori parte protensa': Reg. x. 80, 20 June 1207.

be genuine[1]. Even the most precisely regulated Chancery must be liable to occasional lapses, and Innocent's judicial mind drew a clear distinction between faults which were fatal and those which arose merely from casual error in details of no moment.

We have noticed the exact fidelity with which the rules of balance and rhythm in the composition of documents were observed in his Chancery[2], and the striking difference in calligraphy between Letters of Grace and Mandates which was now elaborated[3]. Innocent was scrupulous too in the care with which he prescribed the manner in which old and mutilated documents should be recorded. Of this we have only one example, but it furnished a precedent for later Popes. In 1213 the monks of Nonantula presented to Innocent three frayed and tattered Privileges of Hadrian I, Marinus I, and John IX. The Pope ordered a transcript of them to be made, and incorporated it in a Bull ratified by his seal, so that the monastery might possess an authoritative exemplification[4] of its title-deeds. His Scriniarius caused all that could be recovered from

---

[1] 'Nullum in eis signum falsitatis vel suspicionis invenimus nisi paucarum litterarum rasuras, quae nequaquam sapientis animum in dubitationem vertere debuerunt': Reg. i. 405, 20 Oct. 1198; inserted in the Decretals, v. xx. 9. Before Innocent's time this had been laid down by Alexander III: 'Dicimus quod propter abrasionem illam [litterae] iudicari falsae non possunt, nec etiam haberi suspectae, praesertim cum et privilegia in possessionibus abradantur et litterae in narratione facti (si erratum est) possunt incunctanter abradi': Decr. II. xxii. 3.   [2] Above, pp. 94 f.

[3] Above, pp. 115–118, 121 f.; cf. Appendix v.

[4] This later English term corresponds to the phrase used by Innocent, 'iussimus fideliter exemplari.'

the papyrus writings, which had in part perished
by reason of their great age, to be set out in the
form of a notarial Act; and the Pope supplied by
the help of the context portions which were presumed to have existed in the originals when
perfect. These conjectural insertions were written
for distinction in a peculiar handwriting, *tonsis
litteris*[1]. 'Shorn letters' was the name given to
the character derived from the Half-Uncial which
had formed itself in the British Isles and passed
back to the Continent in the Carolingian time[2];
it was the same type of writing as that which was
introduced in a modified form into the opening
line of the Papal Bull in the eleventh century[3].
The restoration was confined to syllables or
portions of words where there was practically no
doubt as to the reading. If there was a larger
lacuna a space was left in the transcript.

This single illustration shows how Innocent III
anticipated the methods of the modern critical

[1] 'Ea quae de ipsis scriptis papyriis ex quadam parte prae
nimia vetustate consumptis colligere potuit, in publicam formam
redigere procuravit: quibus nos, apostolici favoris praesidium
impendentes, in hac pagina fecimus sub bulla nostra conscribi,
supplendo quaedam quae secundum litterae circumstantias in
integris praesumebantur originalibus fuisse descripta, quae causa
discretionis mandavimus in hac charta tonsis litteris exarari':
Reg. xvi. 61, 13 June 1213.

[2] See L. Traube, Perrona Scottorum, in Sitzungsberichte der
philos.-philol. und der hist. Classe der K. B. Akademie der
Wissenschaften zu München, 1900, pp. 534–537.

[3] See Delisle, Les 'Litterae tonsae' à la Chancellerie Romaine
au xiiie Siècle, in Bibl. de l'École des Chartes, lxii. (1901), 256–
263; where a facsimile is given of a Bull of Gregory IX presenting
similar features. Another specimen of the same pontificate will
be found in Mittheilungen, xxv. (1904), 291 f.

editor, just as in his examination of suspected documents *in stylo et filo, charta et bulla*[1] he laid down the principles which remain to this day the foundations of diplomatic study. The features in his all-embracing activity to which I have drawn attention serve to complete the picture which I have attempted to draw of the exactness and perfection with which his Chancery was regulated. After his time the standard he had set was in most respects long maintained, though the rules of the Cursus were by degrees less strictly observed. But to give even a summary account of the later medieval system, with its constantly increasing elaboration of procedure and routine, would lead me far beyond my limits. I conclude with some passages from a famous poem on the State of the Roman Court, which describes the Chancery as it was during the pontificate of Urban IV[2].

[1] Reg. VII. 34.

[2] This poem was printed by Flacius Illyricus and by Mabillon from different texts. It has been recently edited by Professor Hermann Grauert, in an exhaustive work entitled Magister Heinrich der Poet in Würzburg und die Römische Kurie, which was published in the Abhandlungen der Königlich Bayerischen Akademie der Wissenschaften, philos.-philol. und hist. Klasse, xxvii. 1, 2 (1912). My quotations are taken from this edition. The poem in some manuscripts is assigned to Geoffrey de Vino Salvo (*fl.* 1200), but it is certainly of a later date than his time. The attribution to Master Henry is given in a Würzburg MS of the poem, and is confirmed by the statement of Hugh of Trimberg, who wrote in 1280: see his Registrum multorum Auctorum, p. 41, ed. J. Huemer, 1888. It is placed beyond doubt by Dr Grauert's minute examination of all the evidence. He dates the composition of the poem in the time of Urban IV (1261–1264): see pp. 410 f. I may notice that Dr Grauert is in error in supposing that the Bodleian MS. Auct. F. 1. 17 contains this poem as well as the Poetria nova of Geoffrey.

Ut multe cernuntur apes in vallibus Ethne   215
   Sic ope multorum Curia fulta viget.

Writers of Petitions.

Sunt ibi qui norunt formare negocia quevis,

Draughtsmen.

   Et sunt qui formas abreviare sciunt.

The number of Writers.

Scriptorum numeri non clara mente recordor,
   Sed mihi cum quadam nube venire solent.   220
Nec facile esset, eos numero deprendere certo,

They engross the draughts, and the fair copies are returned for collation.

   Sed possunt decies, ut reor, esse decem[1].
Istorum labor est cartas grossare notatas
   Et grossas cameris restituisse suis.

Notaries submit Petitions to the Pope.

Sunt ibi qui referunt[2] sacri Pastoris ad aures   225
   Ardua vota hominum sollicitasque preces...
Protinus expediunt quicquid datur expedien-
      dum   233
   Et mora sollicitos non tenet ulla viros.
Festinant urgentque die noctuque labores   235
   Inceptum donec perficiatur opus.
Res quandoque datur tribus expedienda diebus
   Quam tamen instanter expedit hora brevis.

The Petition is drawn up

Prima dies igitur scribet quodcunque petendum

and presented;

      est   240

then the Letter is engrossed and sealed.

   Et tua portabit vota secunda Patri.
Tercia grossabit, bullatum quarta videbit
   Et potes in quinta dicere, Roma vale....

[*Should a document be rewritten,*]

The Corrector Litterarum Apostolicarum.

Hoc Correctoris factum dependet in arte,   270
   Qui iubet ut redeat carta sapore novo.
Ille tibi apponet per se vel demet, amice,
   Rem quam non poteras consuluisse tibi.

---

[1] Under Clement V they were about 110: see his order of 27 October 1310, in Tangl, Päpstliche Kanzlei-Ordnungen, pp. 82 f.

[2] Hence when Petitions came to be entrusted to a distinct class of officials, these were called Referendaries: see below, Appendix vii. 2. Compare Dr R. von Heckel's Commentary, in Grauert, p. 216.

Ille oculus tuus est, et ne qua parte vacillet
    Res tua subtili lumine lustrat opus....   275
Ille mihi quidam faber esse videtur et ipsos   281
    Fabrorum ritus officiumque sequi.
Si producta nimis sit littera, ponit in ignem
    Ingenii et crebro verbere curtat opus:
Si brevis est et eget ut sit producta, favillas   285
    Excitat et rursus massa sub igne calet;
Malleus eductam tandem sic corripit illam,
    Longius ut crescat, amplificetque viam....

[If objection be taken,]

The Auditor Litterarum Contradictarum.

Contradictarum certus sedet arbiter illic,   319
    Officio cuius discucietur opus.
Si res est simplex et non preiudicat ulli,
    Expediet cursus absque labore suos.
Si vero talis fuerit quod forte gravari
    Inde potest aliquis, altera forma subit.
Tunc sub dissimili ponetur iudice causa,   325
    Nec poteris ventis ad tua vota frui.
Sic etenim servat sua Curia iura cuique,
    Ne quisquam vere possit ab Urbe queri.
Cum fuerit concors convencio facta, repente
    Mittitur ad bullam carta refecta sacram....   330

[Of the Vice-Chancellor.]

The Vice-Chancellor

Ille secunda manus Pape est, mediaque diei   345
    Pondus et estatis parte levare solet....

brings Litterae legendae before the Pope.

Huius et hoc opus est et regula certa legendas   351
    Ut ferat ante Patrem, cum vacat hora,
        sacrum.
Plus aliis candoris habens hec ultima fornax
    Fervet et ad purum quodque reducit opus....

[*But Petitions may be rejected by the Lector[1] without being thus presented.*]

The Lector may reject Petitions.

Omnia longinqui cognovit temporis usu   435
    Que Pater admittit, queque negare solet:
Ne sacras igitur teneat sermonibus aures
    Et det inutilibus tempora multa sonis,
Cassat eas quas Papa preces transire vetaret,
    Quam cito prodiret primus ab ore sonus.   440
Que vero retinent formam cursumque probati
    Tramitis, hec[2] numquam supprimit, ymo
        legit....

[*After an account of the Cardinals and of the Pope, we are introduced to the Bullator.*]

The Bullator.

Venerit ad bullam perfecte pauper et exul;   999
    Promeruisse potest forte salutis opem.
Alter ab excelso si sit transmissus Olympo:
    Ni prius enumeret munera, litus arat.
Bulla reclamatur si non in tempore certo,
    Dentibus horrendis dilaceratur opus;
Et nisi legales sint et sine crimine nummi,   1005
    Littera de bulla nulla sequetur eos.

---

[1] At this date he was a Notary, but not much later his place was taken by a Referendary: see Bresslau, i. 683 f. (1st ed.).

[2] So corrected by Mabillon; Dr Grauert prints *hos*.

APPENDIX

I. The Liber Pontificalis[1]

In the thirteenth century the earliest portion of the Liber Pontificalis was supposed to be the work of Damasus[2], because it opens with a correspondence between St Jerome and that Pope; but these letters are known to be spurious, and no section of the existing book can be assigned to so early a date. In modern times scholars went to an opposite extreme and attributed the whole of the first part, ending late in the ninth century, to Anastasius, the papal librarian of that time. This opinion does not go further back than Panvinio and Bellarmin about 1600: it was refuted by Schelestrate so long ago as 1692[3], but nevertheless, through force of repetition, it continued to hold its ground even until recent years[4]. The only dispute now is whether the book, as a book, was compiled in any of its existing forms in the sixth or the seventh century. But in this book, as we have it, are imbedded earlier materials which carry back its evidence as far as the middle of the fourth century and indirectly further still.

The oldest elements of which the book is composed are two lists of Popes. One of these is contained in a chronological collection known as that of the Chronographer of the

[1] See above, p. 5.

[2] Thus Martin of Troppau says that he compiled his Chronicle *ex cronicis Damasi pape de gestis pontificum* and from other works: Monumenta Germaniae historica, Scriptores xxii. 407.

[3] See Duchesne's introduction to the Liber Pontificalis, i. (1886), p. xxxv.

[4] In Migne's Latin Patrology the book is printed among the works of Anastasius in volumes cxxvii., cxxviii. (1853, 1852).

year 354[1], which was drawn up on the basis of an earlier list in 336 and revised during the pontificate of Liberius (352–366): this is distinguished as the Liberian Catalogue, or, from the name of the illuminator of Pope Damasus, who may have been its scribe, the Catalogue of Filocalus[2]. The second ancient source is the Catalogue, preserved only in a number of derived copies, which is called by Bishop Lightfoot the Leonine Catalogue[3] and is assigned by him and by Monsignor Duchesne[4] to the fifth century: Mommsen, on the other hand, who styles this text the Index, claims for it an antiquity equal or superior to that of the Liberian Catalogue[5]. From these two lists, for the earliest time chiefly from the Liberian, the compiler of the Liber Pontificalis drew the skeleton of his work.

At what date this was put together scholars are not in agreement[6]. The record ending with the death of Pope Felix IV (526–530), known as the Catalogus Felicianus, is regarded by Waitz and Mommsen as the nucleus out of which the developed work grew, while Monsignor Duchesne holds that it is an abridgement of an older form of it[7]. According to Monsignor Duchesne the original work was compiled early in the sixth century; it was begun perhaps under Hormisdas (514–523), and in its first form completed after the death of Felix IV. The compiler of the original work, Monsignor Duchesne infers from the vernacular style, was a Papal notary attached to the administrative department of the

---

[1] Printed by T. Mommsen, Chron. min. (Monum. Germ.), i. 73–76 (1891), and by C. Frick, Chron. min., i. 123–129 (1892).

[2] Duchesne, i. pp. vi.–x.

[3] The Apostolic Fathers, I. i. 311 (1890).

[4] Introd., § iii.

[5] Liber Pontificalis, i. (1898), proleg., p. xxix., in Monum. Germ. This edition at present extends only to the pontificate of Constantine (708–715).

[6] A useful summary of the questions in dispute as to the origin and composition of the Liber Pontificalis is given by A. Brackmann in Herzog and Hauck's Realencyklopädie für protestantische Theologie und Kirche, xi. (1902), 439–446.

[7] Duchesne, i. pp. xli.–xliii., xlix.–liv., lviii., lxiv.

Lateran Palace, probably to the Vestiarium or Wardrobe, rather than to the Chancery. He was acquainted with archives containing rescripts of Popes, but the only documents from which he has made extracts are the endowments of pious foundations, which he seems to have taken from some sort of chartulary[1]. The great bulk of the information he gives—and the same thing may be said of his continuators[2]— relates to matters which came within the province of the Wardrobe. It does not concern the Papal finances or ordinary expenditure, but with the Pope's 'privy purse' outgoings, his bounty[3]. The original work was added to while the Goths still ruled Italy, and the notices of the Popes between 530 and 537 are the work of a contemporary[4]: after this latter date an interval elapsed before the record was resumed, probably in the last quarter of the century, and its notices are meagre and of small value. These additions were made either by stages or at a single bound in the course of the seventh century[5]. Waitz[6] and Mommsen[7], on the other hand, consider that the finished work even in its first recension was not composed until the early part of the seventh century, after

---

[1] Duchesne, i. pp. clxii., cf. cxlv. *b*, clii. *a*.

[2] Cf. *ibid.*, p. ccxliv.

[3] *Ibid.*, p. ccxliii.

[4] *Ibid.*, pp. xxxvi.–xlviii. This portion of the work Monsignor Duchesne (pp. ccvii., ccxxxi.) considers to represent a second edition of it made towards the middle of the sixth century. It has come down to us in at least two different classes of manuscripts, and the text has undergone a good deal of redaction and interpolation.

[5] First there are the lives of Pelagius II and of Gregory the Great, and then those of Gregory's five successors down to 625. After this, with Honorius I, begins a series of lives apparently composed in most instances one by one, though sometimes several lives seem to be the work of a single writer. By the middle of the seventh century there are signs that the biography might be begun in the Pope's lifetime, and this was certainly the case in the eighth: Duchesne, pp. ccxxxiii., ccxxxiv.

[6] See his two papers in Neues Archiv, iv. (1879), 217–237, ix. (1884), 459–472.

[7] Liber Pontificalis, i. proleg., pp. xiii.–xviii.

the death of Gregory the Great[1], and that the second recension was not made until after the death of Pope Conon[2] (687).

From this time onwards continuations were made to the book extending to the death of Pope Constantine (715)[3], to Stephen II (757), Stephen III (772)[4], and Hadrian I (795). The narrative now possesses the value of a strictly contemporary record. The Life of Hadrian was probably written as far as chapter xliv in 774, the very year of which it gives the narrative[5]. Its sequel presents a new text, which is continued with greater or less amplitude down to late in the ninth century; but the manuscripts languish, and end abruptly either in the third year of Hadrian II in 870, or after a gap of three pontificates with a fragment concerning Stephen V[6].

This is really the end of the book as a collection of Lives. For the period following we have nothing but jejune Catalogues for two hundred years, from the accession of John VIII in 872 down to that of Gregory VII in 1073[7]. They tell us a few personal particulars about each Pope, but only occasionally, as in the case of John XII, do they contain any regular historical narrative. From the accession of Gregory VII to the pontificate of Honorius II, that is from 1073 to 1130, the case is very different. Here we have substantial if brief Lives of each Pope, written for the most part by contemporaries and containing a variety of valuable details. They were put together and the last three of them composed by one Pandulf, a subdeacon at Rome who did his work some time after 1133, perhaps after 1137. All this later part, from Hadrian II to Honorius II, is contained in a manuscript written in 1142 by

---

[1] Mommsen admitted the existence of an earlier recension of the book, ending with Felix IV, but he held that it had perished and was only represented by epitomes.

[2] An abridgement ending with this Pope exists and is known as the Catalogus Cononianus: Duchesne, i. pp. liv.–lvii.

[3] *Ibid.*, pp. ccvii.–ccxix.

[4] *Ibid.*, pp. ccxxv., ccxxvi., ccxxxiii.

[5] *Ibid.*, p. ccxxxvii.

[6] *Ibid.*, ii. (1892) 195 f., and intr., pp. ii.–viii.; compare above, p. 36.

[7] *Ibid.*, pp. xiii.–xx.

Peter surnamed William, librarian of the monastery of St Giles
on the Lower Rhône[1]. Of the Lives at the beginning there are
other manuscripts, and of the Catalogues which follow them
there are variant texts; but Peter William's book is the only
one which contains the Lives from Gregory VII onwards.

It is usual to append to these two great sections of the
Liber Pontificalis a continuation made by Cardinal Boso
which is contained in the Liber Censuum of the chamberlain
Cencius written in 1192 in a manuscript which still exists at
the Vatican[2]. But it is only in part a continuation. It starts,
like the Liber Pontificalis itself, with St Peter and is for the
greater part of its range a compilation from it. But it becomes
of great importance in the twelfth century, ending with the
Life of Alexander III. Subsequent collections of Lives are
of a different character and composition, and come from
different sources: they cannot be ranked as parts of the
Liber Pontificalis[3].

II. The Regions of Rome[4]

That there were at various times three different sets of
regions in the city of Rome is not disputed; and another was
formed by the modern regions which only ceased after the
overthrow of the Pope's temporal government. The three
older systems were:

1. The fourteen ancient or civil regions established for
the purpose of administration by Augustus;

2. The seven ecclesiastical regions which served the needs
of the Christian Church and are traced back to the third
century;

3. The twelve later or medieval regions, the origin of
which has long been a subject of controversy.

The first question to answer is, which of these three series
is denoted by the numbers assigned to particular regions in

---

[1] Duchesne, ii. pp. xxiv.–xxxvii.　　[2] *Ibid.*, p. xxxvii.
[3] Monsignor Duchesne prints them down to the pontificate
of Martin V: *ibid.*, pp. 449–523.　　[4] See above, p. 8.

historical works and documents. H. Jordan, a most learned
investigator of the topography of ancient Rome, laid down
that all numbered regions which we find mentioned down
to the twelfth century are civil regions. They correspond
roughly, if we disregard textual mistakes and inaccuracies, to
the districts mapped out by Augustus, with the single exception
that from the seventh century onwards the XIIIth region is
called the Ist, while no evidence exists concerning the ancient
Ist, Xth, and XIth[1]. There is, Jordan maintained, no
foundation for the view that the Liber Pontificalis or even
perhaps the letters of Gregory the Great refer to any other
regions than these: 'the seven ecclesiastical regions served
for titles for the clergy but were not applied as designations
of localities[2].' In other words the Deacons and Notaries
were arranged in regions, but these regions were not used with
a precise topographical denotation.

Jordan's opinion, it will be seen, requires the emendation
of inconvenient statements, which are treated as scriptural
errors. But, what is more important, it ignores the plain
fact that, if the city was divided among certain officials for
ecclesiastical purposes, this involved the formation of local
districts. It is true that no unequivocal example has been
found of an ecclesiastical region cited by number with a
definite local attribution. An inscription of the year 338
commemorating a Lector of the second region[3], though it
may raise a presumption, does not prove that that region was
the second ecclesiastical one[4]; and the references in the Liber

[1] Topographie der Stadt Rom im Alterthum, ii. (1871), 317–
321.

[2] *Ibid.*, pp. 326 f. Camillo Re, who agrees with Jordan as to
the continued use of the civil numbers down to the eleventh
century, does not accept his opinion concerning the ecclesiastical
regions: see his paper on Le Regioni di Roma nel Medio Evo, in
Studi e Documenti di Storia e Diritto, x. (1889) 349–363.

[3] J. B. de Rossi, Inscriptiones sacrae Urbis Romae, i. (1857–
1861) 42, n. XLVIII.

[4] As Monsignor Duchesne contends: Notes sur la Topographie de Rome au Moyen Âge, in Mélanges d'Archéologie et
d'Histoire, vii. (1887), 397 f.

Pontificalis to St Clement's church as in the third region[1] would be equally applicable to either system of numeration. On the other hand, when the Liber Pontificalis states, as it usually does, that a Pope was born in such or such a region, it can only mean that the regions denoted definite localities, and the fact that no region bearing a higher number than seven is mentioned leaves no doubt that the regions are those of the ecclesiastical series[2].

Monsignor Duchesne asserts in opposition to Jordan that the civil regions passed into desuetude, at least in ordinary use, after the Gothic wars of the sixth century, and that the ecclesiastical regions took their place[3]: if ever after that time a civil region is mentioned, it is merely a piece of antiquarian pedantry[4]. Except in such cases, any reference to a region with a number higher than seven indicates not a civil region, but a region of the later, medieval system. I venture to think that Jordan was right in maintaining the persistence of the ancient numbers for certain purposes, but clearly wrong in denying the employment of numbers to indicate the localities of the ecclesiastical regions; and that, while Monsignor Duchesne was right in insisting on this latter point, he adopted an unnatural interpretation of the evidence in order to prove the disappearance of the civil regions.

Now it is beyond doubt that the ancient regions ceased to be applicable to the conditions to which Rome was reduced

[1] Lib. Pontif., i. 443, 505.

[2] There is, indeed, one instance of a reference to the eighth region printed in the edition of the Liber Pontificalis in the notice of Benedict VI (972, *ibid.*, ii. 255), but it is found only in a variant text of the Papal Catalogue preserved in one manuscript written at the end of the eleventh century (the Codex Estensis: see Liber Pontif., i. p. cxcix.): the explanation added that it was *sub Capitolio* shows that the region belongs to the civil series; Monsignor Duchesne's attempt, in his paper on Les Régions de Rome au Moyen Âge, in Mélanges d'Archéologie et d'Histoire, x. (1890) p. 141, to connect it with the region Campitelli of the medieval system appears unsuccessful.

[3] *Ibid.*, p. 128.   [4] *Ibid.*, p. 135.

after the sack by Totila in 547; *post quam devastationem*, in the fearful words of the Continuator of Marcellinus[1], *quadraginta aut amplius dies Roma ita fuit desolata ut nemo ibi hominum nisi bestiae morarentur*. When the city was repeopled it was inhabited in new parts and whole districts were left derelict. The extent of the change is indicated by the facts that of the first thirteen regions of the ancient system ten, extending from the south to the centre, the east, and the north-east, correspond roughly to three of the later medieval regions, and that the fourteenth seems to have almost passed away out of mind[2]. The ancient regions now meant nothing for the administration of the city, but they continued to be used as a means for identifying property; and thus we find them frequently mentioned in charters of the tenth and eleventh centuries[3]. Possibly they were mechanically repeated from older title-deeds, just as in English leases of the seventeenth century we may read of a tenement bounded by another 'in the occupation of John Stokes,' though John Stokes had been dead for a hundred years.

But as Rome slowly recovered from the disasters of the Gothic wars it became necessary to organize the city for the purpose of defence, and to this we may with probability attribute the origin of the twelve medieval regions. Monsignor Duchesne suggests that this system was imported from the East; it was connected with the Byzantine military system and was introduced into Rome in the seventh century:

[1] Chron. min. ii. 108, ed. Mommsen (Monum. Germ. Hist.) 1893.

[2] I have already noticed (pp. 11 f.) that not one of the *diaconiae* was fixed in this region, the district beyond the Tiber. When this region emerged once more, it was known by its ancient number, XIV: see Gregorovius, iv. 456, note 2. The fourteenth region *trans Tiberim* is mentioned in a bull of John XVIII of 29 March 1005: Pflugk-Harttung, Acta ii. 57, n. 93.

[3] I need not cite the instances which I had collected, as abundant specimens are given by M. Halphen, Études sur l'Administration de Rome au Moyen Âge (1907), in the notes to pp. 8 f. Cf. Gregorovius, iii. 530, note 2.

and thus the establishment of the *scholae militiae*, here as at Ravenna[1], led to the creation of a new series of regions based upon a different principle from either of the older ones. But there is a link between the ecclesiastical and the medieval systems. In the Roman Ordines preserved in texts which go back to the eighth and ninth centuries the clergy and the civil population are found grouped by ecclesiastical regions[2]. There were seven Crosses carried in processions and these Crosses were connected with the regions. For military purposes standards were needed, and in 1143 there is record of twelve standards. This account of the object for which the medieval regions were constituted, though the defective nature of our materials forbids us to assert it as proved[3], furnishes an adequate and reasonable explanation of their distribution. If the system was first constructed in the seventh century, it is likely that the violence of later times led to the modification of its arrangement. Above all, the plunder of Rome by Robert Guiscard in 1084 caused a displacement of

---

[1] Ravenna was divided into twelve regions: one for the church and eleven *bandi* arranged for military purposes: Agnellus, Liber Pontif. Eccl. Ravennat., CXL. p. 370 (Script. Rer. Langobard., ed. Waitz, 1878). These *bandi* were known by their numbers: *ibid.*, XXXIX. p. 303, LXXVII. p. 330. Cf. Charles Diehl, Études sur l'Administration Byzantine dans l'Exarchat de Ravenne (1888), pp. 308 ff.

[2] Monsignor Duchesne thinks (Les Régions de Rome, pp. 142 ff.) that the ecclesiastical regions were parcelled out at a date subsequent to the ninth century to suit the shifting of the population, and that their place was taken by the eighteen *diaconiae*. See too his note to the Liber Pontificalis, ii. 253.

[3] The argument which has been drawn from the Life of John XIII, to show that the 'mean folk' in 965 was organized under twelve *decarcones*, does not seem to be warranted by the text: 'De vulgo populo qui vocantur decarcones duodecim suspendit in patibulo,' Liber Pontif., ii. 252, and Duchesne's note on pp. 253 f. Cf. Giesebrecht, Geschichte der Deutschen Kaiserzeit, i. (5th ed., 1881) 874 note 3. The document on which Re relies for the existence of fifteen regions in 964 (pp. 365 f.) is a well-known forgery: see Monum. Germ. Hist., Leg. II. ii. 168 ff., Jaffé, Reg. 3705.

population which probably made a re-grouping of the regions necessary. The district from the Lateran Palace to the Colosseum was consumed by fire, and the Coelian and Aventine hills were gradually abandoned[1]. The number of regions required for the south and south-east became smaller, while there became a greater need for organization of the rapidly growing districts to the north-west and along the Tiber. But the twelve regions of the city are positively attested in 1118, when on the occasion of the election of Gelasius II we read of *regiones duodecim Romanae civitatis, Tiberini, et Insulani*[2]. The regions included only the parts within the walls: the Transtiberine district with the Island lay outside[3]; it was not comprised among the regions until the thirteenth century.

The discussion of the relation of the three systems of regions has been greatly confused by the assumption, which has been taken for granted by many writers, that the medieval regions bore numbers, like the ancient and the ecclesiastical systems. There was no more reason why they should bear numbers than, for instance, the wards of the city of London. As a fact they were mentioned simply by name, exactly as we speak of the Ward of Cornhill. If ever a number is added, it is an ancient number supplied for the purpose of topographical identification[4]. It appears from an addition to the Mirabilia Urbis Romae contained in a manuscript written between 1220 and 1226[5], that even then the arrangement of the regions was not completely settled. We there find mention first of the fourteen civil regions; then of the system of seven cohorts guarding the regions in pairs[6]; and finally, *postquam Romana est virtus attenuata et*

---

[1] Cf. Gregorovius, iv. 251 ff.   [2] Liber. Pontif., ii. 313.

[3] This fact is an evidence of the early date at which the medieval regions were formed: cf. above, pp. 11 f., and Halphen, p. 15, note 2.

[4] Halphen, p. 13 and note 5; Duchesne, Les Régions de Rome, p. 146.

[5] Cod. 1180 of the Imperial Library at Vienna.

[6] Referring to the title De officio Praefecti Vigilum, in the Digest, I. xv. 3: 'Septem cohortes opportunis locis constituit, ut binas regiones Urbis unaquaeque cohors tueatur.'

loca mutata et nomina transformata, et sic duodecim principales regiones in urbe sunt ordinate, qui divise sunt in viginti sex[1]. It is of these twenty-six not of the twelve that he gives the names and numbers; and his list includes not only the Transtiberine district but also the Leonine City. The first clear evidence that the regional system crossed the Tiber is quoted from the fourteenth century[2], but the regions were not reckoned in an official numerical order until the time of Martin V[3]. At length in 1586 the Borgo or Leonine City was admitted as the fourteenth region.

The following table gives the names of the regions as arranged by authority under Martin V, with their numbers (A)[4], followed by the slightly different order of numeration found in a Turin catalogue of the fifteenth century (B)[5]. In the last column (C) I print an entirely different series of numbers found in Spruner's Atlas[6], of which I have not explored the origin; it is stated to represent the distribution of the regions after the pillage of Robert Guiscard. On the left hand I have set down the numbers of the civil and ecclesiastical regions, not in the least in order to suggest even a rough approximation to a comparison,—for the different systems did not, and were not intended to, correspond,—but simply in order to indicate in the most general way the immense disparity of area included in each[7].

[1] Re, p. 372.

[2] *Ibid.*, p. 375.

[3] *Ibid.*, p. 376; Duchesne, pp. 146 f.

[4] Re, p. 377; also in Kehr, Regesta Pontificum Romanorum, i. pp. vii.–ix.

[5] Cod. Lat. 749, printed by F. Papencordt, Geschichte der Stadt Rom im Mittelalter (1857), p. 53; cf. Re, p. 371. This numbering is given by Gregorovius, iv. 620, and Halphen, p. 10.

[6] Hand-Atlas zur Geschichte des Mittelalters und der neueren Zeit (3rd ed. by F. Menke, 1880), plate xxii. From this the numbers are repeated in my Historical Atlas of Modern Europe (1902), plate lxix.

[7] I must add that, partly through repeated tracing of maps and copying out of lists of figures, and partly through defective eyesight, I fear that these two columns are not free from error.

CIVIL	ECCLES.	Regio	A	B	C
II, III, IV, V }	iii, iv	Montium et Biberaticae	1	1	2
VI }		Trivii et Viae Latae	2	2	3
VII		Columnae et S. Mariae in Aquiro	3	3	4
		Campi Martis et S. Laurentii in Lucina	4	4	5
		Pontis et Scorticlariorum	5	5	6
IX	v, vi	Parionis et S. Laurentii in Damaso	6	8	12
		Arenulae et Caccabareorum	7	7	11
		S. Eustachii et Vineae Tedemarii	8	6	13
		Pineae et S. Marci	9	9	14
II, IV, VIII, X, XI	ii, iii	Campitelli et S. Adriani	10	12	1
IX	v	S. Angeli in Foro Piscium	11	10	10
I, XII, XIII	i	Ripae et Marmoratae	12	11	9
XIV	vii	Transtiberim	13	13	8
...	...	[Burgi]	14	14	7

III. SALUTEM ET APOSTOLICAM BENEDICTIONEM[1]

It has often been asserted that the Greeting in the form *Salutem et Apostolicam Benedictionem* is found as early as the time of John V and Sergius I at the end of the seventh century. For this Mabillon adduced evidence from the documents of the abbey of St Benignus at Dijon[2], and gave facsimiles of parts of the two Bulls[3]. He did not however take these from the originals. The papyrus, he says, had so much perished that it became necessary for the documents to be restored, *recognosci, approbari, ac in integrum restitui*; and this was done by official authority in 1663[4]. Mabillon duly noted that one of the Bulls contained an error in the Indiction, but he expressed no further suspicion of their genuineness[5]. The authors of the Nouveau Traité de

[1] See above, p. 23.
[2] De Re Diplomatica (ed. 1709), p. 622. [3] Tab. XLVI.
[4] P. 36. This record was acquired by the Bibliothèque Impériale at Paris in 1867. It is printed in full by Delisle, Mélanges de Paléographie et de Bibliographie (1880), pp. 37–43.
[5] Mabillon, p. 436. Delisle notes (p. 45) that, a little before Mabillon, Le Cointe had condemned the Bull of Sergius as a forgery.

Diplomatique[1] followed him in defending the documents, and drew attention to their importance not merely as containing the formula in question, but also as proving that a Bibliothecarius was employed in the Papal Chancery at that early date and that it was not necessary to insert the Imperial year in the Datum: that a Datum should appear at all or that a Pope of the seventh century should have inserted his Pontifical year does not seem to have caused surprise. It was not until Jaffé published his Regesta Pontificum Romanorum in 1851 that the Bulls were definitely set down as spurious[2]. After him Delisle discovered evidence which proved that they were forged some time after 995[3]. Previously the documents had been known only from facsimiles. Delisle examined three fragments of the actual Bulls, two at Dijon and one which had been stolen by Libri[4]. He discovered that the papyrus leaves on which these letters, professing to emanate from the Chancery of two different Popes, were written contained on their backs portions of a single Privilege of John XV dated on 26 May 995. The forger could not procure new sheets of papyrus and had to make use of a sheet already written on. No proof could be more complete.

If these forgeries misled scholars for many ages, an invention of a different sort not only carried back the use of the formula to the earliest days of Christianity, but succeeded in embodying the statement of its authorship in the Roman Breviary. In the eleventh century a fashion arose of adding a special interest to the lives of different Popes by attributing to them an individual share in the composition of the Liturgy

---

[1] v. 148 ff.

[2] Doubts had indeed been expressed by Bréquigny and Gaetano Marini: see Delisle, p. 46.

[3] Mélanges, pp. 47–52. He had already given reasons for regarding the documents with extreme suspicion in his Notice sur un Papyrus de la Bibliothèque de Lord Ashburnham, in Bibliothèque de l'École des Chartes, 6th series, iii. (1867), 455–466.

[4] This last is now restored not to Dijon, but to Paris, Nouv. Acquis. Lat. 1609: see Delisle's Catalogue des Manuscrits des Fonds Libri et Barrois (1888), p. 57.

and in the establishment of particular ordinances. Bonizo of Sutri in the fourth book of his Decretum assigns to a number of early Bishops of Rome successive stages in this work. Thus St Clement *instituit canonem super Eucharistiam ante quam frangatur decantari*; St Alexander inserted the passage beginning *Qui pridie*. Other Popes appointed regulations of other sorts: Evaristus *constituit ut septem diacones essent in urbe Roma qui custodirent papam ne infestaretur a malivolis*[1]. Martin of Troppau, better known as Martinus Polonus, who repeated these statements, finding that no special claim was made for St Cletus—a Bishop whose existence is more than doubtful—supplied the defect thus: ' Hic pontifex invenitur primus posuisse in litteris suis *Salutem et apostolicam benedictionem*[2].'

The lesson for St Cletus on 26 April may be found in an undated Breviarium secundum consuetudinem Romanę Curię, said to have been printed at Venice in 1505. It is taken verbally from the Liber Pontificalis, except that the length assigned to his episcopate[3] does not agree with any known text. In Cardinal Quignon's first revision of the Breviary published in 1535[4], and in his second edition of 1536[5], the lesson is different; it is abridged from Platina's work De Vitis Summorum Pontificum[6], but the mention of the epistolary formula is not yet found. It appears however in Johannes Stella's Vite ducentorum et triginta summorum Pontificum, 1507, in a narrative which is compiled from Martin of Troppau as well as from Platina: 'Primus litteris apostolicis *Salutem et apostolicam benedictionem* scripsit.' The reformed Breviary of Pius V follows closely the text of the Liber Pontificalis, but inserts in the middle of it a sentence and

[1] A. Mai, Nova Patrum Bibliotheca, VII. iii. 32, 1854.

[2] Monum. Germ. hist., Script. xxii. 410.

[3] 'Annos .vii. mensem unum dies .xi.' Cf. H. Kellner, in Historisches Jahrbuch, xxxiii. (1912), 109.

[4] Breviarium Romanum a Francisco Cardinali Quignonio editum, ed. J. Wickham Legg (1888), p. 125.

[5] The Second Recension of the Quignon Breviary, ed. J. Wickham Legg, i. (1908), 276.

[6] Pp. 9 f., ed. 1626.

a half apparently derived from Stella, in which we read, according to a copy printed at Venice in 1623, 'Primus in litteris verbis illis usus est, *Salutem et Apostolicam benedictionem*[1].' The source of the statement was believed both by Monsignor Pierre Batiffol[2] and by Suitbert Bäumer[3] to be unknown, but it is manifestly derived either from Martin of Troppau or from Stella. Since I ascertained this fact I have found that it was already pointed out by the Bollandists so long ago as 1675[4].

IV.   The Judices Palatini[5]

Two descriptions of the Roman Judices have come down to us in somewhat blundered forms. One has been called the Notitia of c. 1000 and the other the Fragment of c. 1000; but both of them are apparently incomplete, and as they are generally accepted as belonging to the time of Otto III, and as the shorter fragment is of a glossarial character, they may be conveniently distinguished as the Ottonian Notitia and the Ottonian Gloss. Of these the Gloss has by far the earlier manuscript attestation[6]. It is found in a volume in the

---

[1] It may be noted that this sentence is not contained in Breviaries published at Avranches (1733), Evreux (1737), Amiens (1746), Chalon (1765), Paris (1778), Chartres (1783), Vienne (1783), Rennes (1787), Langres (1830), Besançon (1834), or Laon (1839). But it appears in that published at Cologne in 1718, and I am informed that it held its position in the authorized editions until recent years. I find it, for instance, in a Breviary printed at Lyons in 1846. I have not undertaken a systematic examination of the matter; I merely cite the editions which I have inspected.

[2] In Bulletin Critique, 1892, p. 15.

[3] Geschichte des Breviers, 1895, p. 432.

[4] Acta Sanctorum Aprilis, iii. 411.   [5] See above, p. 51.

[6] See the accounts of the manuscripts given by Dr S. Keller, Untersuchungen über die Judices sacri Palatii Lateranensis, ii., in the Deutsche Zeitschrift für Kirchenrecht, x. (1901), 187–203, and by M. Louis Halphen, Le Cour d'Otton III à Rome, in Mélanges d'Archéologie et d'Histoire, xxv. (1905), 354 note 4.

Laurentian library at Florence, Cod. Aedil. cxxii., which was written about the year 1000 and formerly belonged to the Cathedral Church. This contains a Gregorian Sacramentary, followed, according to Bandini[1], by a group of *ritus et orationes ad consecrandum Episcopum, ad coronandum et benedicendum Imperatorem*, then our Gloss, *Missa in ordinatione Pontificis*, and other masses, *ordines*, and prayers. The Gloss next appears in a series of compilations of the last quarter of the twelfth century: (1) the Liber politicus (polyptychus) of Benedict Presbyter, Cambray MS 554; (2) the Gesta pauperis scholaris Albini, Cod. Ottobon. 3057; (3) the Liber Censuum of Cencius the Chamberlain, afterwards Honorius III, Cod. Vatic. Lat. 8486[2]. It is also inserted in the Graphia aureae Urbis Romae and in the Liber de Mirabilibus Urbis Romae, two surveys of the City which assumed their present shape about the middle of the twelfth century; but of these the Graphia is preserved only in a manuscript of the thirteenth or fourteenth century[3], and the Mirabilia has no earlier text than that given by Cencius[4]. Still, though their manuscript transmission is unsatisfactory, it is probable that one or the other of them in its original form was the source from which Benedict, Albinus, and Cencius derived their copies of the Gloss.

Now, although the Mirabilia can in fact be traced back nearly to 1143, while the Graphia, as we have it, is not older than about 1154, the Graphia is in fact of a considerably

---

[1] Biblioth. Leopold. Laurent., i. (1791), 214 *b*, 215.

[2] Dr Keller, p. 192, thinks that, though Cencius made use of Albinus, he did not derive his text of the Gloss from him, but either from the Graphia or the Mirabilia.

[3] Florence, Biblioth. Laurent., lxxxix. infra, cod. 41, whence it was published by A. F. Ozanam, Documents inédits pour servir à l'Histoire littéraire de l'Italie (1850), pp. 155–183.

[4] Le Liber Censuum de l'Église Romaine, ed. by P. Fabre and L. Duchesne, i. (1901), 262–273. Montfaucon first printed the work from a manuscript of the thirteenth century: Diarium Italicum, ii. 283–298 (1702). It gives a text of the Gloss (pp. 289 f.) similar to that of Albinus.

earlier origin[1]. It consists of three parts. The first is a
short historical introduction, beginning with the Tower of
Babel[2]; this is peculiar to the Graphia. Secondly, it describes
the classical topography of Rome and its Christian monuments
in a treatise[3] which in form and content shows a considerable
general affinity and often verbal agreement with the parallel
description in the Mirabilia, but the order of the sections in
the two works differs a good deal. It is only in this part of
the Graphia that we meet with statements written in the
twelfth century[4], and these few notices are plainly interpo-
lations. The third part introduces a new subject with the
words, *His itaque prelibatis, nomina et dignitates illorum qui
in excubiis imperialibus perseverant describamus.* It sets forth
the manner in which the Imperial Court was organized at
Rome, according to the author's account, in his time, and
it enumerates the Judices not as Papal but as Imperial
officers. This section of the Graphia[5] is independent of the
Mirabilia. It is in part derived from the Origines of Isidore
of Seville, and shows a connexion, though not perhaps a
close connexion, with the work of the Emperor Constantine
Porphyrogenitus De Ceremoniis Aulae Byzantini[6]; but it
also includes not only the Gloss but three formulae which are
found also in the Vatican MS 4917 of the eleventh century.

These features lead to the conclusion that the Graphia in its
original shape was composed in the time of Otto III, who was
the only Emperor of the German line who kept a fixed court
at Rome and who is known to have surrounded himself with

---

[1] We may see this from a comparison of the local descriptions:
for instance, 'Theatrum Neronis iuxta monumentum Adriani
imperatoris' in the Graphia, p. 159, becomes 'Theatrum Neronis
iuxta castellum Crescentii' in the Mirabilia, ap. Lib. Censuum, i.
263 *b*.

[2] Pp. 155 f., ed. Ozanam.   [3] Pp. 156–171.

[4] Thus p. 163, 'In monumento vero porfiretico beate Helene
sepultus est Anastasius iiii papa,' gives the latest date, 1153.

[5] Pp. 171–183.

[6] This connexion, if accepted, excludes Ozanam's attribution
of the Graphia to the period between the sixth and the eighth
centuries, probably about 663: p. 91. Cf. Keller, p. 195.

that Byzantine ceremonial which the Graphia describes[1]. This is the view taken by Wilhelm von Giesebrecht[2], who accounts for the absence of the later sections of the work from the Mirabilia on the ground that, since the Western Emperors no longer had their residence at Rome, these descriptions ceased to have more than an antiquarian interest and were therefore omitted. The earlier, topographical part however continued to be transcribed, and came to form the nucleus of the Mirabilia. Giesebrecht admits the paradox that the part of the Graphia which relates the establishment of the Christian court of Otto III should bear a purely pagan aspect. He thinks the author may have been a grammarian, more occupied with antiquities and etymologies than with the actual condition of things[3]. While however the third part of the Graphia was thus omitted in the Mirabilia, the little fragmentary Gloss about the Judices was inserted, without regard to arrangement, between the legend about the Marble Horses and the mention of the Column of Antoninus[4].

An examination of the text of the Notitia leads to a similar conclusion as to the date of its composition; but the manuscripts in which it is preserved are not so early[5]. It is found (1) in the historical compilation which Bonizo of Sutri prefixed to his Decretum, printed by Cardinal Mai, Nova Patrum Bibliotheca, VII. iii. 59 f. (1854[6]), by F. Bluhme,

---

[1] In addition to the often quoted passages describing Otto's attempt to revive the old Empire, reference may be made to a lawsuit of 999 set out in the Farfa chartulary, iii. 149 ff., in which we read of the *praefectus navalis*, the *vestararius sacri palatii*, and the *imperialis palatii magister*.

[2] Gesch. der Deutschen Kaiserzeit, i. 5th ed. (1881), 879 f.; cf. Gregorovius, iii. 517 ff.   [3] Cf. Keller, p. 200.

[4] Liber Censuum, i. 272. It is not however included in the late twelfth-century text of the Mirabilia prefixed to the Chronicle of Romuald of Salerno in the Vatican MS 3973, and printed by C. L. Urlichs, Codex Urbis Romae topographicus (1871), pp. 92–112.

[5] A careful account of the manuscripts is given by Keller, pp. 161–164.

[6] The discovery of this work is an interesting piece of literary history, which does credit to the critical acuteness of Pertz. See

in the Monumenta Germaniae, Leges, iv. (1868) 663 f., and by Giesebrecht, i. 893 f.[1]; (2) in John the Deacon's Liber de Ecclesia Lateranensi, dedicated to Alexander III and printed by Mabillon, Museum Italicum, ii. 570 (1689)[2]; (3) in Godfrey of Viterbo's Pantheon, printed in Waitz's edition in the Monumenta Germaniae, Scriptores, xxii. (1872) 304.

In all three texts the Notitia is inserted in a context with which it has no organic connexion. Bonizo gives it in a collection of miscellanies. In John the Deacon it follows an interpolated inscription of 1297. Godfrey inserted it in his second edition (MSS of the class D) which was dedicated to Gregory VIII (1187), and omitted it in his third. Bonizo and Godfrey give a longer text than John the Deacon, but we need not hesitate to follow Giesebrecht[3] and Dr Keller[4] in regarding the concluding part of the longer recensions as an addition, probably made by Bonizo. John must therefore have had access to an earlier and to this extent an uncontaminated text.

But the earlier part also presents difficulties. If we accept the enumeration of the judices as a Roman document, the question at once arises whether the interpretations of the terms *scriniarii = tabelliones,* and *defensores = advocati,* do not point to a redaction by a writer familiar with the officials of Ravenna. Dr Keller goes further and by an acute analysis of the grammar and structure of the whole arrives at the conclusion that the Roman Notitia is imbedded in a Ravennate account of the judices of that city; so that the latter is interrupted between 'Alii pedanei a consulibus creati' and 'Alii vero qui dicuntur consules' by the insertion of this older

Keller, l. c. Some confusion has arisen from the fact that G. B. de Rossi, who first transcribed the text, omitted to copy the sentences after 'et ideo fallitur.'

[1] Giesebrecht originally published it in his first edition of 1855.

[2] The pagination of the edition of 1724 agrees with this. The Notitia is given in chapter viii, but the next chapter is numbered xii. It does not appear from what manuscript Mabillon published his edition; it cannot have been of a date earlier than the fourteenth century.

[3] i. 881.   [4] Pp. 166 f.

matter. I have indicated this by printing what appears to be the original Notitia in italics; but I am not sure that the insertion of the Notitia has not produced a further disturbance in the statement about the judices at Ravenna which cannot now be amended. Nor is it clear whether the text of the Notitia begins, as I have printed it, with 'Septem sunt iudices' or with the clause preceding, but I incline to think that this clause is due to the redactor. Dr Keller is of opinion that the existing form in which the Notitia appears, as redacted at Ravenna, may be dated between 1010 and 1090[1].

I reprint side by side the Gloss from the Laurentian manuscript as given by Bluhme in the Monumenta Germaniae, Leges, iv. 663, with selected variants from Keller, pp. 202 f.; and the Notitia from Giesebrecht's copy of Bonizo with various readings from Godfrey of Viterbo. These I take from the editions, as I have not had the opportunity of collating the manuscripts myself. I have rearranged the order of the officers in the Gloss so as to agree with that in the Notitia, but have numbered them as they stand in the manuscripts.

---

[1] P. 179.

The Ottonian Gloss.

Incipit de VII grad[ibus] quomodo nominantur apud Grecos et Latinos[1]. Primicerius[2] id est prima manus. Chera[3] Grece Latine manus dicitur.

---

[1] Instead of this incipit Albinus and Cencius give a title, *De nominibus iudicum et eorum infractionibus.* I take the variants of A (and C where it differs) from Dr Keller, pp. 202 f.
[2] *Primicerus* C.
[3] A ins. *enim.*

The Notitia.
Quot sunt genera iudicum.
Iudicum alii sunt palati[1], quos ordinarios vocamus; alii consules, distributi per iudicatus; alii pedanei, a consulibus creati[2]. In Romano vero imperio et in Romana usque hodie aecclesia[3] *septem sunt iudices palatini, qui ordinarii nominantur,*

---

[1] *Palatini* Godfrey, Bonizo (ed. Mai).
[2] G adds *id est nostri iudices.*
[3] Some MSS of G have *in Romana vero ecclesia* omitting *In Romano vero imperio et.*

The Ottonian Gloss.

Primicerius apud Grecos papia[1] vocatur. Ipse debet habere clavi de
toto palatio[2] et esse ibi honorabilis
apud imperatorem, die noctuque in
palatio debet esse[3].
II. Secundicerius id est secunda
manus. C[hera] G[rece] L[atine]
m[anus] d[icitur]. Et[4] apud Grecos
secundicerius[5] vocatur depterus. In
palatio honorabilis est, et ibi [debet]
esse die noctuque[6], et[7] coronae et
omn[ium] vestiment[orum] imperi-
ali[um][8] qu[ae] per festas[9] indu-
[untur], ipse debet habere curam.
V. Arcarius[10] debet[11] colligere
censum.
VI. Saccellarius[12] debet habere
curam monasteriorum ancillarum
Dei, et in festis[13] debet introducere
omnem honorem[14] ante imperatorem.
VIII. ¡Protoscriti, protoscriniarius[15].

The Notitia.

*qui[1] ordinant imperatorem et cum
Romanis clericis eligunt papam.
Quorum nomina haec sunt: Primus
primicerius. Secundus qui dicitur
secundicerius. Qui ab ipsis officiis
nomen accipiunt. Hi dextra levaque
vallantes imperatorem, quodammodo
cum illo videntur regnare; sine
quibus aliquid magni non potest con-
stituere imperator[2]. Set et[3] in Romana
aecclesia in omnibus processionibus
manuatim ducunt papam, cedentibus
episcopis et ceteris magnatibus, et in
maioribus festivitatibus octavam super
omnes episcopos legunt lectionem.
Tertius est archarius[4], qui praeest
tributis. Quartus saccellarius[5], qui
stipendia erogat militibus, et Rome
sabbato scrutiniorum[6] dat elemosinam,
et Romanis episcopis et clericis et
ordinatis viris largitur presbiteria[7].
Quintus est protus[8], qui praeest
scriniariis,* quos nos tabelliones vo-

---

[1] The παπίας had the keys of the
Palace: see J. J. Reiske's note to
Constantine Porphyrogen. de Ceri-
moniis, ii. 39 f. (ed. 1830).
[2] *curam de clavibus totius palatii* A.
[3] *Existere debet* A.
[4] *C G L m d Et* om. A.
[5] Om. A.
[6] *Et nocte* A, *et noctu* C.
[7] Om. A.
[8] Om. A. Compare Reiske's
note on the σακελλάριος, ubi supra,
ii. 156.
[9] *festivitates* A.
[10] *qui ab archano dicitur* ins. A.
[11] *scire secreta consilia imperatoris et* ins. A.
[12] *Sacellanus* A.
[13] *festivitatibus* A.
[14] *omnem honorem* om. A.
[15] *Protoscriti protoscriniarius* om.
A, who inserts *Protoscriniarius id
est primus scriniariorum* before
Bibliothecarius.

[1] Keller suggests *quia*.
[2] G *papa*.
[3] *etiam* v.l. in G.
[4] *arcadius* G.
[5] *cellerarius* G.
[6] *infirmorum* v.l. in G.
[7] *id est a prebendo* add. G.
[8] *id est primus* add. G.

The Ottonian Gloss.

IV. Primus defensor[1], apud Grecos protohecdico[2] vocatur. Ipse[3] debet habere homines sub se, qui defenda[n]t sedem imperii, ubi residet in ecclesia[4].

III. [Nome]nculator Latine, apud Grecos questor dicitur. Ipse debet habere curam de viduis et orphanis et omnibus xenodochiis, et apud ipsum[5] debet disputari de testamentis.

VII. Bibliothecarius apud Grecos logothetis[6], referendarius interpretatur, quia[7] ipse debet renuntiare omnem scriptionem ad imperatorem[8].

---

[1] A ins. *latine.*
[2] *prohecdicos* A.
[3] Om. A.
[4] A om. the last four words.
[5] *eum* A.
[6] *logothenus* A.
[7] *interpretatur quia* om. A.
[8] In the Graphia (Ozanam, pp. 172 f.) the text after *ad imperatorem* proceeds with sentences on the *Kymiliarchus, Consules, Proconsul, Dictator,* and *Patricii,* which have nothing corresponding to them in A.

The Notitia.

camus. *Sextus primus defensor, qui praeest defensoribus, quos nos advocatos[1] nominamus. Septimus amminiculator, intercedens pro pupillis et viduis, pro afflictis et captivis. Hi pro criminalibus non iudicant[2], nec in quemquam mortiferam dictant sententiam, et Rome clerici[3] sunt[4], ad nullos umquam alios ordines promovendi.* Alii vero, qui dicuntur consules, iudicatus regunt et reos legibus puniunt et pro qualitate criminum in noxios dictant sententiam.

[5] Ceterum postquam peccatis nostris exigentibus Romanum imperium barbarorum patuit gladiis feriendum, Romanas leges penitus ignorantes inliterati ac barbari iudices, legis peritos in legem cogentes iurare, iudices creaverunt, quorum iudicio[6] lis[7] ventilata terminaretur. Hi accepta hac[8] abusiva potestate, dum stipendia a republica non accipiunt, avariciae face succensi ius omne confundunt. Comes enim inliteratus ac barbarus nescit vera a falsis discernere et ideo fallitur. Qui si mente pertractarent illud propheticum, Iuste iudica proximo tuo, et non accipies in iudicio personam pauperis nec honores vultum potentis, mallent ab omni munere manus excutere, quam per cecam animi cupiditatem inlecti Dei se facere reos esse iudicio, dicentis, Qua mensura mensi fueritis, remetietur vobis. Set et Romanis legibus rei habentur ac notabiles, qui abusive ad libitum leges inflectentes non iudicant ex equitate, sed propria voluntate. Hi dati sunt aecclesie in adiutorium, ut qui non reverentur episcopos pro aecclesiastica disciplina, saltim per horum terrorem et gladios ad pacis, licet inviti, redeant unitatem.

---

[1] *advocatum* v.l. in G. [2] *nondum dicunt* G.
[3] *domini* v.l. in G. [4] G prefixes *qui.*
[5] What follows is found only in Bonizo and Godfrey.
[6] *iudiciorum* G. [7] *lex* B G. [8] Om. B.

V. A Formulary of the Thirteenth Century[1]

The following short list of rules for the drawing up of Letters of Grace and Mandates has been several times published. It was first printed by Delisle in 1858 in his Mémoire sur les Actes d'Innocent III[2] from the Paris MS Lat. 4163, written towards the end of the thirteenth century. Then in 1890 Simonsfeld, who was ignorant of Delisle's edition[3], published another text from a very bad manuscript of about 1400 at St Mark's, Venice. Cl. IV. Lat. n. 30[4]. Six years later he discovered a third manuscript, written between 1363 and 1371, at Munich, Cod. Lat. 17788, and produced another edition which took account of all three manuscripts[5]. Simonsfeld used the Munich manuscript as his basis, and gave a collation of the Paris and Venice texts. I have preferred to adopt the earlier text of the Paris manuscript (P), printed by Delisle, and to distinguish the additions of the Munich manuscript (M) by square brackets. I therefore retain Delisle's numeration of the paragraphs, which have been used for reference by other scholars. Though in a text like this no exact reproduction of the forms of the documents can be attempted, I have introduced a heavy type as a rough representation of the ornamental forms given in Simonsfeld's facsimile of the Munich manuscript. I have

---

[1] See above, pp. 117 f.

[2] Bibliothèque de l'École des Chartes, 4th series, iv. 23.

[3] This ignorance and the slovenliness of Simonsfeld's edition provoked a severe and just reproof from Dr Tangl, in Mittheilungen, xii. (1891) 189 f.

[4] Beiträge zum päpstlichen Kanzleiwesen im Mittelalter, in Sitzungsberichte der philos.-philol. und hist. Classe der k. B. Akademie der Wissenschaften zu München, 1890, ii. 255 f.; cf. pp. 228–231.

[5] Neue Beiträge zum päpstlichen Urkundenwesen im Mittelalter, in Abhandlungen der historischen Classe der k. B. Akademie der Wissenschaften, xxi. ii. (1896) 365 f. Other manuscripts are mentioned by Dr Tangl, *ubi supra*, and in Deutsche Zeitschrift für Geschichtswissenschaft, viii. (1897), Monatsblätter 5–6, pp. 158 f.

not noted variations of spelling or transpositions of words, nor have I inserted any readings from the Venice MS (V).

The Formulary comes from the Audientia Litterarum Contradictarum, a department of the Chancery in which, at least as early as the time of Innocent III[1], Letters were examined before they were registered and passed on to the parties interested[2]. Though the oldest manuscript is as late as the pontificate of Boniface VIII, the practice which it records goes back in most points nearly a century earlier[3]. It would appear that the strict regulation of the minutiae of the writing of Letters was brought in under Alexander III and thenceforward gradually developed. It was part of the process by which Letters of Grace took over decorative features from the Privilege. Under Alexander III we note that the Pope's name is written in full, without abbreviation (art. 2), and that distinctive capitals introduce the clauses *Nulli ergo* and *Si quis* (art. 7)[4]. It was also in his time that the Datum came to be spaced out so as to fill up nearly the whole of the last line of the document[5]. The elegant tittle (*titulus*) to mark contractions in Letters of Grace (art. 5) seems to have been introduced into them under Celestine III. By his time also the employment of capitals for the initials of proper names had become uniform[6]. M. É. Berger, the editor of the Registers of Innocent IV, asserts that the

[1] See the references to it in the Chronicon Abbatiae de Evesham, pp. 145, 199.   [2] See Bresslau, i. 281 f.

[3] The details for the time before Innocent III have been explored by Kaltenbrunner, in Mittheilungen, i. 405–409; those for Innocent III by Delisle, in his Mémoire; and for Innocent IV by M. É. Berger, Les Régistres d'Innocent IV, i. (1884) pp. l., li.; and those from the middle of the thirteenth century by Diekamp, in Mittheilungen, iv. 502–505.

[4] From his time also *apostolicam* in the Greeting is far more commonly written with *-cam* than with *-cā*; but 7 for *et* may still be found in it beyond the middle of the thirteenth century.

[5] This feature is not mentioned in our rules.

[6] This rule was probably established earlier, but it was not always observed, *e.g.*, by the Antipope Calixtus III. See an example of its neglect in 1169, in Spec. 111 n. 28.

rules printed below are exactly followed in the originals of that Pope. But the prohibition of certain marks of contraction (art. 8) was only strictly observed in Letters of Grace, and the rule about the arrangement of the elements in the Datum (art. 11) was at no time uniformly adhered to. The general inference to which an examination of the Formulary leads us is that it is founded on a set of rules compiled at the beginning of the thirteenth century and partially revised to suit modifications of details which were made during its course. It was the elaboration of the first line and the gradual emphasizing of the initials of the main sections of the document which came, as time went on, to mark the Letter of Grace from the Mandate in a manner which cannot be mistaken. The large ornamented initials of such words as *Dilecto, Iustis, Sane, Nulli, Siquis,* at once strike the eye; but the calligraphy was so obvious that it formed a poor protection against forgery. Hence it was thought expedient to devise more intricate technicalities which could not be so easily learned.

Letters with silk and Letters with string.

In Letters with silk the Pope's name is written tall, with an ornamental initial, the remaining letters being of full height with or without floriation.

The initial of the Address has a tall initial.

The Greeting.

In all Letters the initial of the following word is written large, but in Simple Letters it is an ordinary majuscule.

1. Est notandum quod littere domini pape alie bullantur cum serico, alie cum filo canapis.

2. Que autem cum serico bullantur debent habere nomen domini pape [per omnes litteras] elevatum, prima semper apice[1] existente et facta cum aliquibus spaciis infra se, reliquis litteris eiusdem nominis de linea ad lineam attingentibus, et cum floribus vel sine eis, hoc modo **Bonifacius** ep̊s[2] etc. Et ubi dicitur *Dilecto filio,* D debet elevari hoc modo : **Dilecto** etc.

3. *Sat et apticam*[3] *ben̄* in omnibus sic scribitur.

4. Littera autem prime dictionis que immediate sequitur *ap.*[4] *ben.* debet semper magna esse in omnibus litteris, puta sic, **Ad** audientiam etc., nisi in simplicibus[5] ubi debet esse mediocris, isto modo, Conquestus [est] etc.

---

[1] Delisle (p. 24) explains this as meaning *prima littera semper cum apice.*
[2] Delisle prints *episcopus.*
[3] So M: *Sal't et apc̄a* P. See above, p. 189 note 4.   [4] PM *ad.*
[5] That is. in Letters *in forma communi*; cf. Delisle, p. 22.

In Letters with silk abbreviations in proper names are usually indicated by a tittle; in Letters with string, always by a plain stroke.

In Letters with silk there are ligatures between *s* and *t* and *c* and *t*.

Nulli ergo and *Siquis* each begin with a large tall initial.

Not all signs of contraction are permitted.

[Letters must not be ruled.]

The parchment must be without a hole or obvious mend.

[*Nulli ergo* must not be inserted in Indults.]

[The word preceding the Date must not be divided between two lines.]

5. Item notandum quod in istis litteris cum serico titulus debet esse super nominibus, ut supra factus est in ep͞s¹, hoc modo ৪² vel alias³ ut placebit scriptori, non tamen in omnibus⁴. In illis autem cum filo canapis semper planus hoc modo [-].

6. Item notandum quod in litteris cum serico quando *s* attingit *t* [ex parte ante in eadem dictione *t*] debet aliquantulum prolongari ab *s*, hoc modo, teſtimonium, etc.⁵ Illud idem fit de *t* cum coniungitur ad *c* in eadem dictione, hoc modo, dileƈto, etc.⁶

7. Item notandum quod *N* de **N**ulli ergo, etc., et *S* de **S**iquis autem, etc., semper in omnibus litteris, ubi scribuntur, debent⁷ esse magne et elevate, ut hic, et maiores, ut forme competet⁸.

8. Item nota quod in litteris papalibus non recipiuntur omnes breviature, ut iste ꝑ, [q3,] ꝓ⁹, et hiis similes, nec tale 2¹⁰.

[Item nota quod littere pape non debent lineari cum plumbo vel cum incausto: quod si fieret essent suspecte.]

9. Item [nota] quod in nulla parte sui¹¹ debent continere foramen vel suturam¹² apparentem¹³.

[Item nota quod in litteris indulgentiarum non debet esse Nulli ergo etc., et si ponatur littere sunt rescribende, tamen sunt cum filo serico.

Notandum quod dictio que est ante datam littere non debet dividi, sed poni tota in uno latere: verbi gratia, *per* in uno latere et *hibere* in alio.

---

¹ Delisle prints *epistolis*.   ² P S.   ³ M *aliter*.
⁴ Diekamp observes (p. 503) that the use of the tittle ৪ is here prescribed only over proper names, and that the plain stroke may be found over other words; in the Avignon period the latter was used with proper names too.
⁵ *etc*. om. M.
⁶ It is not here denied that these ligatures may also be found on Letters with hemp, but according to M. Berger they do not appear under Innocent IV. Diekamp observes (pp. 503 f.) that in such Letters the form of ligature, where it occurs in the second half of the thirteenth century, is of a plainer type than that on Letters with silk.
⁷ *debeant* M.   ⁸ *competit* M.
⁹ *p*[*ro*], *p*[*er*] P. Diekamp (p. 504) emends *pre* for *per*.
¹⁰ The sign for *ur*: M and V have 7, the sign for *et*.
¹¹ *sui*: *dicte littere* M.   ¹² *scisuram* M.
¹³ *apparenter* M. This paragraph is omitted in V.

[In Letters directed *ad instar*, the Pope's name must be written in tall compressed characters.]

[In Litterae Simplices, if the Text fills two parts of the line, the whole Date must be in the same line; if it fills three parts, that of the pontificate may be in a second line.]

[In a recital of an ancient Privilege which has decayed the name of the Pope must not be in large letters.]

In Letters sealed on string the initial only of the Pope's name must be tall;

Dilecto filio must begin with a capital.

In all Letters the Date must be complete in one or two lines,

but the date of the month must not be divided between two lines.

Proper names and names of offices and dignities must have capital initials.

Item est sciendum quod, quando in littera dicitur *ad instar*, littere debent[1] esse levate vel inherentes in nomine pape, hoc modo, **Clemens**, et sic in aliis.

Item in simplicibus litteris tenendum est quod in ultima linea, [si] sunt duo partes tantum, data tota debet esse ibidem; et si sunt ibidem tres partes, tunc pontificatus esse poterit in secunda linea.

Item nota quod quando aliquod privilegium propter vetustatem petitur renovari et dicatur propter nimiam vetustatem consumptam, et inseratur in litteris alterius pontificis, littere in nomine pontificis debent esse parve, sic : Innocentius etc.[2]]

10. Item nota quod ille littere que bullantur cum filo canapis debent habere primam litteram nominis domini pape elevatam et reliquas communes, hoc modo **Bonifacius**, etc. Ubi dicitur[3] *Dilecto filio*[4] *d* debet esse tale **D** vel tale D seu huius[5] forme, et sic de similibus.

11. Item nota quod in omnibus litteris apostolicis data tota debet esse in eadem[6] linea vel[7] in duabus, ita quod [*Datum Laterani* sit semper in una linea, vel] *Datum Laterani Kal. Ianuarii* sit in una linea, et *Pontificatus nostri anno septimo* sit in alia. Quod si secus fieret, littere essent corrigende; scilicet, si *Dat. Laterani kalendis* essent in una[8] et quod sequitur in alia[9], vel e contrario : vel forte suspecte essent.

12. Item nota quod in litteris apostolicis omnia propria nomina personarum, locorum, nomina officiorum et dignitatum debent habere primam litteram elevatam, sic, *Petrus, Canonicus, Episcopus*, et similia.

---

[1] MS *debet.*

[2] These five paragraphs are absent both from P and V.

[3] *dicit* M.   [4] *dilectis filiis* M.

[5] *talis* M.   [6] *una* M.

[7] For *vel* the Paper Register of Clement VI reads *non*, representing the older rule : see Tangl, in Deutsche Zeitschrift, *ubi supra*, p. 159.

[8] *una linea* M.

[9] *alia linea* M.

[Nowadays the word *Data* may end a line and the name of the place may begin a new one.]

Dates are given by nones, ides, and kalends.

[Item nota quod *data* tenetur modo in una linea et *Avinionis* in capite alterius, sed hoc sustinetur in illis in quibus †non[1] est[2].]

13. Et quia hic de data est mentio, de illa dicatur. Notandum quod data[3] scribitur secundum nonas, secundum idus, et secundum kalendas mensium[4].

---

[1] *nō* MS. Simonsfeld extends *nomen*, but the text is probably defective. Cf. Tangl, l.c. pp. 160 f.
[2] This paragraph is also omitted in V. [3] *datum* M.
[4] In M and V there follows an explanation of the Roman Kalendar.

VI. THE ROMAN PROVINCIALE[1]

A Provinciale or catalogue of sees arranged under provinces was inserted by Albinus, Cardinal Bishop of Albano, in the tenth book of his Gesta[2]. This part of his work was finished after 29 October 1188 and in all probability before May 1189 when he was made bishop[3]. The original manuscript is not known to exist, but we possess a copy which is of very nearly the same date[4]. Albinus however was not the author of the Provinciale. It is true that it includes Monreale (1182), but this is apparently an addition to the list. The omission of Hebron and Petra (1167) indicates an earlier date, while the inclusion of Trondhjem (1154) and Upsala (1164) suggests that it was compiled between 1164 and 1167[5]. Monsignor Duchesne inclines to the opinion that it was drawn up by Cardinal Boso, who was Chamberlain under Hadrian IV and Alexander III[6].

[1] See above, pp. 150 f.
[2] On this book see E. Stevenson, in Archivio della R. Società Romana di Storia Patria, viii. (1885) 357 ff.
[3] Paul Fabre, Étude sur le Liber Censuum de l'Église Romaine, pp. 10 f., 1892.
[4] Codex Ottobonianus Lat. 3057, in the Vatican Library. Either this or the original was formerly in the Papal Archives.
[5] The omission of Carlisle may point to a time thirty years earlier: in this case the list must have been added to as years went on.
[6] Introduction to Liber Censuum (1910), p. 56.

Appendix VI

In 1192 the Chamberlain Cencius, afterwards Pope Honorius III, undertook the composition of a tax-book, the Liber Censuum, in which he gave a list of sees after the manner of a Provinciale, inserting under the different bishoprics the monasteries from which the Roman Church claimed revenue. The skeleton of this list was derived not directly from Albinus but from Albinus' source, presumably Boso. The book is preserved, as it was drawn up under Cencius' direction, in the Vatican MS 8486[1].

The question arises, to what Provinciale Giraldus Cam-

[1] *Ibid.*, pp. 1–7.

Giraldus	*Albinus*
Et cum verteretur ad regnum Anglorum, scriptum in hunc modum ibidem et lectum fuit:	IN REGNO ANGLIE.
	Metropolis civitas Cantuaria has habet civitates sub se:
Cantuariensis metropolis suffraganeas habet ecclesias istas, Roffensem, Londoniensem et caeteras per ordinem.	Lundoniam,
	Rohecestriam
	Cicestriam,
	Cestriam,
	Excestriam,
	Guintoniam,
	Salesberiam.
	Herefordiam,
	Guilicestriam,
Enumeratis autem singulis suffraganeis ecclesiasticis Angliae, interposita rubrica tali,	Bahadam,
	Nicholam,
	Norguicium,
	Helyam,
De Wallia, prosequitur in hunc modum, *In Wallia Menevensis ecclesia, Landavensis, Bangoriensis, et de Sancto Asaph.*	In Gualia vero Menevia,
	Pangoria.
	Landaph,
	et Sanctus Asaph.
	Sunt autem numero XVIII.
	Metropolis civitas Emboracus habet sub se Dunelmum.

brensis refers when he speaks of Innocent III having ordered out such a book in order to verify the statements made about the independence of the Welsh sees[1]. In order to assist us in forming a judgement on this point, I print below side by side, first, the account given by Giraldus, secondly, the list of Albinus[2], thirdly, that of Cencius[3] (omitting the names of monasteries), and, fourthly, a list written not long after

[1] De Iure Menevensis Ecclesiae, ii., in Opera, iii. 165.

[2] Printed by Gaetano Cenni, Monumenta Dominationis Pontificiae (1761), ii. pp. xxvi., xxvii., and at the end of Monsignor Duchesne's edition of the Liber Censuum, ii. 100.

[3] Liber Censuum, i. 223–226.

Cencius	*Bologna MS.*
ANGLIA.	IN ANGLIA.
In archiepiscopatu Cantuariensi.	Archiepiscopatus Cantuariensis hos habet suffraganeos :
In episcopatu Lundoniensi.	Lundoniensem
In episcopatu Rofensi vel Rovecestrensi.	Roffensem sive Rovecestrensem
In episcopatu Cicestrensi.	Cicestrensem
In episcopatu Exoniensi.	Exoniensem
In episcopatu Wintoniensi.	Wintoniensem
In episcopatu Batoniensi et Wellensi.	Bathoniensem
In episcopatu Salesberiensi.	Saresburiensem
In episcopatu Wigorniensi.	Wigoriensem
In episcopatu Herfordensi.	Herefordensem
In episcopatu Conventrensi.	Conventrensem sive Cestrensem vel
In episcopatu Lincolniensi.	Lichifeldensem
In episcopatu Norwicensi.	Lincolniensem
In episcopatu Heliensi.	[Norwicensem[1]]
WALLIA.	Heliensem
In episcopatu Menevensi.	Menevensem
In episcopatu Landavensi.	Landevensem
In episcopatu Bangornensi.	Bangorensem
In episcopatu sancti Asaht.	Sancti Assaph
In archiepiscopatu Eboracensi.	Archiepiscopatus Eboracensis hos habet suffraganeos :
In episcopatu Dunelmensi.	Dunelmensem
In episcopatu Cardocensi.	Cardocensem vel Carleolensem.

[1] Omitted by an evident oversight; the name is found in two later copies of the same list.

1278 and preserved in Cod. 275 of the Spanish College at Bologna[1].

Now Giraldus no doubt was writing from memory, and a verbal agreement with his original is not to be expected. But the main features on which he dwelt were the separation of the Welsh from the English sees by a rubric and the difference of the grammatical construction in the two series. It is at the outset plain that the book consulted was not the Liber Censuum of Cencius, because, although the rubric *Wallia* is retained there, the whole form of the list has been changed: the bishoprics have been turned into the ablative in order to admit of the insertion of monasteries where required; moreover, the province of York is appended carelessly to Wales. In the later (Bologna) list the distinction of the Welsh sees is obliterated, and all are placed uniformly in the same construction as the English; but there are some features in it which suggest that it was derived not from Cencius but from the older Provinciale which was the source of Albinus. If this was the work of Boso, a man well acquainted with England and possibly by birth an Englishman, this would explain the correctness with which the English names are written, as compared with the corrupt forms given by Albinus. And it seems permissible to infer that this older Provinciale was the Register inspected by Innocent III and Giraldus[2].

---

[1] Tangl, Die päpstlichen Kanzleiordnungen von 1200–1500 (1894), pp. 18 f.; cf. introd. pp. lxii.–lxv.

[2] Dr Tangl's supposition (p. xvii.) that it was a book compiled later than the Liber Censuum, that is, between 1192 and 1199, lacks probability. He seems to imply that Albinus' work was superseded by that of Cencius (p. xvi.); but the two were compiled for different purposes.

VII. MISCELLANIES

1. *Bulls on Papyrus*[1].—Dr Bresslau, in the Mittheilungen, ix. (1888) 1–8, enumerates twenty-nine Bulls on papyrus recorded to be in existence in modern times, and M. Henri Omont, in the Bibliothèque de l'École des Chartes, lxv. (1904) 575–582, gives a list of twenty-three actually preserved from the ninth to the eleventh century. Three of the Bulls mentioned by Dr Bresslau have now perished: two at the burning of the abbey of Ripoll in 1835[2], and one at the Louvre in 1871[3]. Thus his total is reduced to twenty-six. But M. Omont adds a Bull of Benedict VIII, making twenty-seven[4]. The difference in the total is accounted for by M. Omont's omission first of the fragment of Hadrian I's Bull, as belonging to a date earlier than the ninth century, and secondly of three small fragments, at Paris, Amiens, and Le Puy. Two of these are unidentified, the third, coming from a Privilege of Leo IX, is remarkable because of its late date[5]. It confirms the fact already known from transcripts made under Gregory IX that papyrus was occasionally used in the Papal Chancery not only under this Pope but even under Victor II[6].

The papyrus was sometimes of enormous length. A Privilege granted by Benedict III to the abbey of Corbie on 7 October 855[7] measures 22 feet 6 inches. It has been often

[1] See above, p. 37.

[2] Omont, p. 575 note 1.

[3] Bresslau, p. 6.

[4] Cf. Bresslau, Handbuch der Urkundenlehre, i. 73 note 2. A shorter list was given with valuable critical remarks by Paul Ewald, Zur Diplomatik Silvesters II, in Neues Archiv, ix. (1883) 327–353.

[5] A facsimile of this last is given by M. Prou, in the Bibl. de l'École des Chartes, lxiv. (1903) 578.

[6] See Marini, I Papiri diplomatici, n. XLIX., L., pp. 84, 86. The terms in which Gregory on 29 July 1236 ordered the Bulls to be exemplified (*exemplari*) will be found in the Registres de Grégoire IX, n. 3544, ii. 587, ed. L. Auvray, 1907.

[7] Jaffé, Reg. 2663.

published from the time of Gaetano Marini[1] onwards, and a reduced facsimile of the entire document was edited by M. C. Brunel for the Société des Antiquaires de Picardie in 1912. Another Privilege of unusual dimensions was granted also to the abbey of Corbie by Nicholas I[2].

2. *The Datary*[3].—The use of the term *Datary* to designate the official who completed the ratification of a Bull by adding the Dating Clause, though admitted by usage, is open to objection because in the later middle ages it came to indicate an official who dealt with an earlier stage in the production of the document. The Petitions on which Letters of Grace were founded passed first into an office known as the Data Communis, and towards the end of the thirteenth or the beginning of the fourteenth century the Notaries who had previously received them were excluded from any share in their examination[4]. A little later the office was called the Dataria, and it was placed under the charge of a Datarius with Referendaries to assist him[5]. When the Petition was approved, the Pope wrote his initials[6] and the official added the Date[7]. In the course of time the functions of the Dataria were amplified, and a greater antiquity was claimed for it[8]. The importance of the Date was recognized also in England in the fourteenth

[1] n. xiv., pp. 17–22.

[2] Mabillon gives its length variously as of nine or seven feet: De Re Diplomatica, pp. 40, 442.

[3] See p. 55.

[4] Bresslau, i. 292 f. (2nd ed.), p. 231 (1st ed.).

[5] *Ibid.*, pp. 683 f. (1st ed.).

[6] *Ibid.*, pp. 738 f. (1st ed.).

[7] A short account of the procedure will be found in Mr Charles Johnson's preface to W. H. Bliss's Calendar of Entries in the Papal Registers relating to Great Britain and Ireland, Petitions to the Pope, i. (1896). Particulars about the work and machinery of the developed office are given by Hinschius, Kirchenrecht, i. § 49 β.

[8] In a seventeenth century manuscript Della Dataria in the Bodleian Library (Mendham MS 35) it is said to go back to the time of Honorius III.

century, when the King's Warrant for the issue of Letters
Patent came to be annotated with a memorandum naming
the Date at which it was received in the Chancery[1]. This
'Livery Clause' gave the Date to be inserted in the Letters,
and was required by Act of Parliament under Henry VI[2].
But no separate office was established, as at Rome, for the
purpose.

3. *The Pope's Name on the Seal.*—It has been said above[3]
that the Seal until Leo IX bears the Pope's name without
his number, and that until Urban II the name is in the
genitive. A detached Seal found in the Forum seems to
anticipate by some months the insertion of the number and
by fifty years the use of the nominative. The legend on the
two sides of this *bulla* is DAMASUS | PAPA II. See De Rossi's
remarks in Atti della R. Accademia dei Lincei, 3rd ser., x.
(1882) 385. The Seal is figured in Dr von Pflugk-Harttung's
Specimina, iii. plate vi. n. 10.

4. *The Points on the Seal[4]*—As the number of points or
beads round the circumference of the *bulla* and on certain
parts of the design on the counterseal served as one of the
criteria of genuineness[5], some details may be given; but the
outer edge of the lead is so often worn or damaged that it is
not always possible to count the number of points round the
circumference with certainty. The obverse, or Seal, of
Innocent II seems to have been surrounded by as many as
ninety-two points; but that of Celestine III had only forty-
nine and Innocent III one less. In the second half of the
thirteenth century Martin of Troppau in his Summa Decreti

---

[1] E. Déprez, Études de Diplomatique Anglaise, 1908, p. 47.

[2] 18 Henry VI, c. 1.

[3] Pp. 119 f.

[4] See above, p. 120.

[5] Conrad of Mure says, 'Circumferentia utrobique certis
punctulis est expressa, ut eo difficilius possit falsificari et eo
facilius falsitas valeat deprehendi': Summa de Arte Prosandl
(written in 1275), in Rockinger, Briefsteller, i. 475.

et Decretalium[1] prescribes seventy-five. But it may be doubted whether much regard was paid to the number of points surrounding this face of the seal, as a new die had to be cut for every pope and many pontificates were not long enough to make the number familiar. With the reverse, or Counterseal, it was otherwise, for the same die might continue in use for a great many years. When the heads of the Apostles were introduced into it by Paschal II in a type the main features of which were preserved until at least the Avignon period, several varying designs were produced, and an old die was not deemed to be superseded by a new one; more than one of Paschal's dies were in fact used by Calixtus II[2]. But when near the end of the pontificate of Innocent II a fresh die was cut, the uniform use of one standard pattern was settled; and thenceforward for a century and a half, with the exception of a short time in 1252 during which an unsatisfactory die was used[3], only six dies are found[4]. The points on these which were counted were as follows[5]:

---

[1] MS. Lat. 4133 in the Bibliothèque Nationale, cited by Delisle, Mémoire sur les Actes d'Innocent III, p. 48 note 1.

[2] See Pflugk-Harttung, Die Bullen der Päpste, pp. 53, 57, and the facsimiles given in Spec. iii., where the mode of their reproduction is not in all respects satisfactory: some are taken from plaster or wax casts, and some from drawings.

[3] Shortly after 8 June 1252 Innocent IV's counterseal was broken while the Pope was at Perugia, and a new die (*typarium*) was made. But it was not successful; according to the Mandate which cancelled it, the heads of the apostles were too coarsely drawn (*corpulentiores solito*). See Delisle, p. 49, and the two Mandates printed on pp. 70 f. The earlier Mandate, of 5 July, authenticating the new seal is calendared in Berger's Registres d'Innocent IV, n. 6771; the second one, cancelling it, bears no date and is not included in the Register.

[4] Dr von Pflugk-Harttung makes the number larger, but for the reasons stated in the preceding note his facsimiles do not enable us to determine the facts.

[5] I take the statistics mainly from Diekamp, in Mittheilungen, iii. 613–626 (with three plates), iv. 530.

Points on	1 12 Mar. 1143—17 May 1155	2 15 July 1155—14 Dec. 1179	3 2 Nov. 1181—29 April 1185	4 30 Mar. 1186—8 June 1252	5 3 June 1253—7 Mar. 1259	6 15 Mar. 1260
Circumference	75?	68 or 69[1]	73	73	73	73[3]
Aureole round the head of St Paul	27	23	25	25	25[2]	24[3]
Aureole round the head of St Peter	29	26	26	26	25[2]	25[3]
Points composing the hair of St Peter's head	—	25	25	25	25	25[3]
Points composing his beard	—	16	28	28	28	28[3]

[1] The specimen is perhaps worn.

[2] Dr L. Schmitz-Rheidt, in Mittheilungen, xvii. (1896) 65, makes the points on the aureoles respectively twenty-six or twenty-seven and twenty-six; but the facsimile he gives is not clear. The numbers however were certainly those given in the table above, as may be seen from the fine reproductions in C. Serafini's Monete e Bolle plumbee pontificie, i. (1910) plate I.

[3] These numbers are those recorded also by Martin of Troppau, cited by Delisle, p. 48 note 1.

5. *Demi-Bulls.*—A Pope elect did not at once adopt the style which was appropriate after his consecration. Gregory VII entitled himself not *episcopus servus servorum Dei* but *Gregorius in Romanum pontificem electus,* and his Greeting was *salutem in Christo Iesu*[1] or *salutem in domino Iesu Christo*[2]. Innocent III's ordination was deferred for more than a month, and during the interval he used only the counterseal of his *bulla.* It is probable that this practice was not new, for the face of the die with the Pope's name required some time to engrave and the business of the Chancery could not be neglected. But Innocent no doubt made a larger use of his power than was customary, for the age and infirmity of his predecessor had left him heavy arrears to overtake. Hence on 3 April 1198 he issued a general rescript confirming them in the following terms:

[1] Reg. I. 1*–11.　　　　　　[2] I. 12.

Quoniam insolitum fuit hactenus ut sub dimidia bulla ad tot et tam remotas provincias litterae apostolicae mitterentur, et ex hoc litterae ipsae diutius quam vellemus possent ex alicuius dubitatione suspendi, ut quorum interest parcamus laboribus et expensis, quae ab electionis nostrae die usque ad solemnitatem consecrationis sub bulla dimidia emanarunt parem cum illis firmitatem obtinere decernimus quae in bulla integra diriguntur[1].

6. *The Closing of Bulls.*—Whether Letters other than *Litterae clausae* were usually tied up before they were dispatched is uncertain, because in most cases the strings protruding from the lower side of the seal have been in part or altogether cut off. But there is evidence to show that the protruding strings were often long enough to pass round the document when folded and then to be tied together[2]. But the supposition that after the middle of the twelfth century the long ends were fastened in the lead at the time of sealing[3] lacks all probability. We know in fact that in the thirteenth century registration took place after the affixing of the seal and that even at a later stage the document might be examined and then cancelled or ordered to be redraughted[4]. It has even been maintained that, besides the double string on which the seal hung, an additional string was used, so that four ends might be enclosed in the lead. This theory seems to be based upon a derelict seal of Innocent IV, preserved at Münster in Westphalia with no document belonging to it, which showed signs of these four ends. Such a mode of sealing looks like an example of the manner of forgery condemned by Innocent III's

[1] Reg. I. 83; cf. Nouveau Traité de Diplomatique, iv. 311.

[2] Thus in a Mandate of Innocent IV in the British Museum (Addit. Charter 20373) the strings are long enough to go round the folded document. In a Letter of Alexander III (Addit. Charter 52148) there are about nine inches of silk protruding, and the same is the case with an Indult of Gregory X (Harleian Charter 111, A. 24).

[3] Diekamp, in Mittheilungen, iii. 610 f., iv. 528 f.; Bresslau i. 960 (1st ed.); R. F. Kaindl, in Römische Quartalschrift, vii. (1893) 492–496.

[4] Tangl, in Mittheilungen, xvi. (1895) 180.

Fourth Rule[1]: it was apparently the case of a genuine seal being attached to a forged document. The same objection seems to apply to the seals which have been noticed[2] where the protruding ends are not those of the original string but two new strings which were tied round the document. In any case we cannot maintain the theory that the long strings were at both ends imbedded in the seal[3].

7. *The Disappearance of the Registers before that of Innocent III.*—With the exception of the Register of Gregory VII, if its character be finally decided, no original Register earlier than that of Innocent III is now preserved, and no reference to any Register of the Popes down to his time is contained after the pontificate of Honorius III[4]. Many of them, from Alexander II onwards, are known to have existed at various dates between the latter years of the eleventh century and the early part of the thirteenth[5]. After that time they disappear and leave no trace. The question therefore has been raised, to what cause we are to attribute the practically total loss of all this great series of volumes. G. B. de Rossi, who gave a valuable history of the places of deposit of the Papal Archives in a Commentatio prefixed to Henry Stevenson's Catalogue of the Palatine Library[6], maintained that some at least of the Registers were stored for safety in the *Cartularium iuxta Palladium*. This he understood to be situate within the limits of the Castle held by the Frangipani, and he urged the constant loyalty of this family to the Popes as a reason for the choice of the Turris Cartularia: when Frederick II granted it to the Annibaldi in 1244 all the documents were destroyed. A closer study of the topography in the light of recent excavation made the first part of this

[1] See above, pp. 154, 155, 156 note 1.
[2] See L. Schmitz-Kallenberg, Urkundenlehre (2nd ed. 1913), p. 96.
[3] See Baumgarten, Aus Kanzlei und Kammer, pp. 191–194.
[4] See Bresslau, i. 109 note 2.
[5] See above, pp. 123 f. and notes.
[6] Codices Palatini Latini Bibliothecae Vaticanae, i. (1886) pp. lxxix.–xcix.

argument more than doubtful[1], and the facts of the relations of the Frangipani to the Papacy in the thirteenth century were fatal to the second[2].

It is however certain that about 1081 Cardinal Deusdedit found some records in this Tower[3]. The important section of his Liber Canonum, iii. 191–207, in which these excerpts are contained includes seventeen pieces, of which fourteen were in the Lateran, and only three in the Cartularium; and these three are definitely stated to have been written on papyrus (*tomi carticii*) and therefore were not Registers of modern date. Apparently they had been taken to the Tower in some time of disturbance, just as when Urban II took refuge there in 1094 he brought some documents with him for reference[4]. In any case there can be no question of the Tower having become the general depository of the Papal Registers. When Giraldus Cambrensis in 1200 consulted the Register of Eugenius III[5] he seems to have found it at the Lateran. Innocent III built a new archive room at St Peter's, but only for volumes and documents required for current business[6]; and he did not continue this arrangement. It may therefore be concluded that the Lateran remained the seat of the Archives down to the time of Honorius III, after which, in circumstances unrecorded, they either were plundered or perished from fire[7].

---

[1] The Tower, which survived until 1829, stood hard by the Arch of Titus; it was no part of the Palace of John VII, which was on the north of the Palatine Hill near the Temple of Augustus.

[2] See F. Ehrle, Die Frangipani und der Untergang des Archivs und der Bibliothek der Päpste am Anfang des 13. Jahrhunderts, in Mélanges offerts à M. Émile Chatelain (1910), pp. 448–485.

[3] Kanonessammlung, III. 191, 193, 194, pp. 353, 357, ed. V. Wolf von Glanvell.

[4] Ehrle, pp. 478 ff.

[5] De Iure Menevensis Ecclesiae, in Opera, iii. 180.

[6] De Rossi, p. xcix.

[7] Ehrle, pp. 481 f.

INDEX

The words Rome *and* Papal *have usually been omitted for the sake of shortness : they must be supplied according to the sense.*